Eat Smart in Turkey

Eat Smart in Turkey

How to Decipher the Menu
Know the Market Foods
&
Embark on a Tasting Adventure

Joan Peterson

Illustrated by S. V. Medaris

GINKGO PRESS, INC

Madison, Wisconsin

Eat Smart in Turkey
Joan B. Peterson

Map lettering is by Gail L. Carlson; insert and cover photographs are by Joan Peterson; photograph of author is by Susan Chwae.

The quote by James A. Michener from "This Great Big Wonderful World," from the March 1956 issue of Travel-Holiday Magazine, © 1956 by James A. Michener, is reprinted by permission of the William Morris Agency, Inc. on behalf of the author.

Publisher's Cataloging in Publication
(Provided by Quality Books Inc.)
Peterson, Joan (Joan B.)
    Eat smart in Turkey : how to decipher the menu, know
the market foods and embark on a tasting adventure /
author, Joan Peterson ; illustrator, S.V. Medaris. --
2nd ed.
    p. cm.
    Includes bibliographical references and index.
    LCCN 95095127
    ISBN 0-9641168-8-X

    1. Cookery, Turkish. 2. Diet--Turkey. 3. Food
habits--Turkey. 4. Cookery--Turkey. 5. Turkey--
Guidebooks. I. Title.

TX725.T8P48 2004   641.59561
                              QBI03-200793
Printed in the United States of America

To Irvin

His love and knowledge of Turkish food
added savor to every page

Contents

The Cuisine of Turkey   1

An historical survey of the development of Turkish cuisine: beginning at the 6th century with nomadic tribes in central Asia, tracing the slow advance of the Turkish people westward across the continent to Anatolia, culminating in modern times.

Regional Turkish Food   15

A quick tour through the seven regions of Turkey to see the diversity of cooking styles encountered in traveling the length and breadth of the country.

Tastes of Turkey   31

A selection of delicious, easy-to-prepare regional and national recipes to try before leaving home.

Preface

> If you reject the food, ignore the customs, fear the religion and avoid the people, you might better stay home. You are like a pebble thrown into water; you become wet on the surface but you are never a part of the water.
>
> — JAMES A. MICHENER

There is no more satisfying way to get immersed in a new culture than to mingle with local people in the places where they enjoy good food and conversation—in their favorite neighborhood cafés, restaurants, picnic spots or outdoor markets. I try to capture the essence of a country through its food, and seek out unfamiliar ingredients and preparations that provide new tastes. By meandering on foot or navigating on local buses, I have discovered serendipitously many memorable eateries away from more heavily trafficked tourist areas. As an unexpected but cherished diner, I have had the pleasure of seeing my efforts in learning the cuisine appreciated by the people in ways that make an understanding of each other's language unimportant.

Each trip energizes me as though it were my first; the preparation for a visit becomes about as exciting as the trip itself. Once I determine the destination, I begin to accumulate information—buying relevant guidebooks, raiding the libraries and sifting through my hefty collection of travel articles and clippings for useful data. A high priority for me is the creation of a reference list of the foods, with translations, from my resource materials. For all but a few popular European destinations, however, the amount of information devoted to food is limited. General travel guides and phrase books contain only an overview of the cuisine because they cover so many other subjects of interest to travelers. Not surprisingly, the reference lists I compiled from these sources were inadequate; too many items on menus were unrecognizable. Some menus have translations but these often are more amusing than helpful, and waiters usually cannot provide further assistance in interpreting them. Furthermore, small neighborhood establishments—some of my favorite dining spots—frequently lack menus and post their daily offerings, typically in the native language, on chalkboards outside the door. So unless you are adequately familiar with food words, you may pass up good tasting experiences!

To make dining a more satisfying cultural experience for myself and for others, I resolved on an earlier vacation to improve upon the reference lists I always compiled and research the food "on the spot" throughout my next trip. Upon my return, I would generate a comprehensive guidebook, making it easier for future travelers to know the cuisine. The book that resulted from that "next trip" featured the cuisine of Brazil and represented the first in what would be a series of in-depth explorations of the foods of foreign countries; to date six other EAT SMART guides have been published. These cover the cuisines of Turkey, Indonesia, Mexico, Poland, Morocco and India. My intention is to enable the traveler to decipher the menu with confidence and shop or browse in supermarkets and fascinating, lively outdoor food and spice markets empowered with greater knowledge.

I have had many memorable culinary experiences while traveling around Turkey. One such experience that greatly enhanced my trip was an impromptu food sampling marathon in Gaziantep, a city in the southeastern region that sees few foreign tourists. What started as a quiet dinner of private discovery in a tiny eatery near my hotel expanded into a "you must try this too!" sort of evening, after a young student waiter learned I was researching the region's specialties and informed the owner. Dish followed dish in an endless stream of local specialties and their many variations. Those dishes in the "must try" category that needed longer preparation time would be available the next day if I were interested. I was! Memorable favorites of these two repasts included *ufak köfte*, a dish of lamb, chickpeas and two different size balls of bulgur in a yogurt sauce. The larger balls were stuffed painstakingly with a mixture of minced meat and nuts after a hole had been poked in them with a finger to create a cavity for the stuffing. An equally delicious version of this dish, with a tart, lemony tomato sauce rather than yogurt, is *ekşili ufak köfte*. Another variation called *yuvarlama* also has flour and water dough balls (*hamur*) about the size of chickpeas. A smidgen of unripe plum paste makes the dish piquant. I acquired the taste for *şalgam*, a drink of beet and carrot juice flavored with lemon, and like the Turks, drank it along with *rakı*, the anise-flavored national liquor distilled from grapes. It is believed that this vegetable juice concoction counteracts the effect of the alcohol. Another interesting drink I sampled was *meyan balı*, an extract of licorice.

A most delicious end to a meal is the sweet treat *künefe*, made with *tel kadayıf*, fine strands of pastry dough resembling shredded wheat. Earlier in the day we had watched these threads being made in special shops. A metal pot containing a liquid flour and water mixture is suspended over a revolving, hot copper griddle. The mixture streams out of little holes at the bottom of the copper pot, making a circular pattern of threads as the griddle turns. They are quickly fried and gathered from the griddle by the handful, forming each time a small bundle of threads. For desserts such as *künefe*, bundles of these threads are soaked in butter and then baked. A layer of cheese is placed between two layers of pastry threads before baking. The dessert is then doused in sugar syrup and served piping hot. Since Gaziantep is the pistachio capital of Turkey, it was not surprising to find a generous sprinkling of these nuts on this delectable dessert.

Everyone confesses both to disliking certain foods and to avoiding others that are unfamiliar. This guide will help steer the traveler away from known problematic foods and will encourage sampling new and unusual ones. The informed traveler will have less concern about mistakenly ordering undesirable food and will, as a result, be more open to experimentation.

The guide has four main chapters. The first provides a history of Turkish cuisine. It is followed by a chapter with descriptions of regional Turkish foods. The other main chapters are extensive listings, placed near the end of the book for easy reference. The first is an alphabetical compilation of menu entries including both typical Turkish fare and specialties characteristic of each of the seven regions of Turkey: the Sea of Marmara region, the Aegean, the Mediterranean, central Anatolia, the Black Sea region, eastern Anatolia and southeastern Anatolia. Outside a particular geographical area, with the possible exception of İstanbul, local specialties are unlikely to be found unless a restaurant features one or more regional cuisines. Noteworthy, not-to-be-missed dishes with country-wide popularity are labeled "national favorite" in the margin next to the menu entry. Classic regional dishes of Turkey—also not to be missed—are labeled "regional classic." The second list contains a translation of food items and terms associated with preparing and serving food. This glossary will be useful in interpreting menus since it is impractical to cover in the *Menu Guide* all the flavors or combinations possible for certain dishes.

Also included in the book is a chapter offering hints on browsing and shopping in the food markets and one with phrases that will be useful in restaurants and food markets to learn more about the foods of Turkey. A chapter is devoted to classic Turkish recipes. Do take time to experiment with these recipes before departure; it is a wonderful and immediately rewarding way to preview Turkish food. Most special Turkish ingredients in these recipes can be obtained in the United States; substitutions for unavailable ingredients are given. Sources for hard-to-find Turkish ingredients can be found in the chapter containing resources. This chapter also cites some groups that focus on travel to Turkey or offer the opportunity to have person-to-person contact through home visits to gain a deeper understanding of the country, including its cuisine.

I would like to call your attention to the form at the end of the book. I would like to hear from you about your culinary experiences in Turkey. Your comments and suggestions will be helpful for future editions of this book. This form can also be used to order additional copies of this book, or any of the other EAT SMART guides, directly from Ginkgo Press, Inc.

iyi yolculuklar, afiyet olsun!

JOAN PETERSON
Madison, Wisconsin

Acknowledgments

We gratefully acknowledge those who assisted us in preparing this book. Irvin C. Schick, Sarah Atış, Murvet Enç, Deniz Balgamış and Nurdan Uyan for translations; Ayla Algar, Hüsnü Atış, Deniz Balgamış, Vedat Başaran, Tom Brosnahan, Holly Chase, Ömer Çeliksoy, Ali Kemal Dinçer, Engin E. Kadaster, Selim S. Kuru, Elizabet Narin Kurumlu, Esra Levent, Christine Ogan, Wynne Oz, Leyla Özhan, Bora Özkök, Gülseren Ramazanoğlu, Irvin C. Schick, Mustafa Siyahhan, Ayşe Somersan, Ressan Süzek, the late Tuğrul Şavkay, Nurten Tabur and Nurdan Uyan for contributing recipes from their private collections; S.V. Medaris for her magical illustrations; Gail Carlson for enlivening our maps with her handwriting; Susan Chwae (Ginkgo Press) for a knockout cover design and classy photograph of the author; Widen Enterprises for the excellent 4-color separations; Michael Kienitz for the super scans and Nicol Knappen (Ekeby) for bringing the text neatly to order.

Thanks also to Leslie Schick for providing invaluable assistance on the history of Ottoman costume, and to Irvin C. Schick, Nilüfer İsvan, Muhtar Katırcıoğlu and Vedat Başaran for insight into historical and comtemporary Turkish menus and cookbooks. We are especially grateful to Irvin C. Schick for editing the manuscript for accuracy of Turkish history and grammar.

We are indebted to many people in the United States and Turkey for help in identifying Turkish regional foods and menu items. In the United States thanks to Irvin C. Schick, Deniz Balgamış, Mustafa Erdem, Ercan Kurar, Selim S. Kuru, Holly Chase, Alice Arndt, Nilüfer İsvan, Wynne Oz, Maria Roselli, Margorie Shaw, Ressan Süzek, Engin E. Kadaster, Ümit Doğan, Gaye Tınaztepe, Shirley Smith, Okyay Çamlıbel, Bora Özkök, Kikuko Yamabe, Paula Dinçer, Tom Brosnahan, Mine Karaçalı, Steve McCormack and Fahriye Sancar.

ACKNOWLEDGMENTS

In Turkey (Istanbul) thanks to Esra Levent and Hans Trautman (IDEE Travel Services), Elizabet Narin Kurumlu and Yavuz Gezmiş (Innovations in Travel), Vedat Başaran (Feriye Restaurant), and Aydın Yılmaz and the late Tuğrul Şavkay, leading food authorities. Thanks also to Esra Levent (IDEE Travel Services) for arranging kitchen tours of the Beyti Restaurant in Florya and the Tuğra Restaurant in the Çırağan Palace Hotel in İstanbul, as well as for arranging a cooking demonstration in the Tuğra Restaurant. In Ankara, Erkal Zenger and Ercan Tunç (Zenger Paşa Konağı Restaurant), Bahadır Kutlu, İsmail Şişman and Adem Kuru (Washington Restaurant) and Shirley Epir (Middle East Technical University). In Nevşehir, Feridun Tabur and Ömer Çeliksoy (Hotel Cappadocia Dedeman); in Gaziantep, Efkan Güllü (Güllüoğlu), Ahmet Kaya (Merak Kimya) and Ahmet Apaydın; in Antakya, Gülden Barutçu and Özden Demirağ (Titus Tourism Agency); in Antalya, İlker Özmaya (Hotel Antalya Dedeman) and in Marmaris, Gwen Bylund, owner of the yacht Hellem Nooh.

We are indebted to the former directors of the US Turkish Tourism Offices, Mustafa Siyahhan (Washington, DC) and Leyla Özhan (New York) for their enthusiasm for this project.

Thanks also to Melody Kyper, Rod Echols, John Mimikakis, Brook Soltvedt, Dave Nelson, Erin Dickerson and Kevin Clark for taste-testing the recipes.

And special thanks to Brook Soltvedt, a most perceptive and helpful editor.

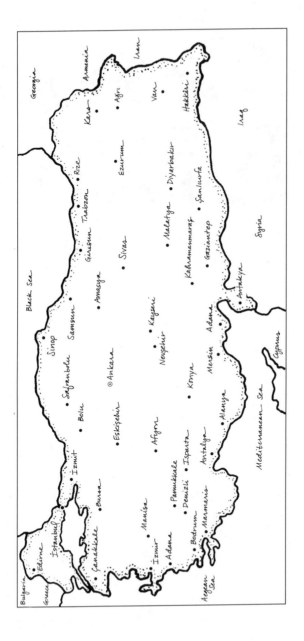

Map of Turkey

The Cuisine of Turkey

An Historical Survey

The Turkish people are descendants of nomadic tribes, who began moving westward from the semideserts of Mongolia and central Asia in the 6th century. Primarily herdsmen, they lived off their flocks and available vegetation. Throughout the slow advance across the continent, they acquired new food practices as they entered the cultural sphere of other kingdoms. Their developing cuisine was influenced by those of China and Persia and, when they arrived in Anatolia, by the Greeks.

Of the many Turkish states known to history, two made major advancements in developing the cuisine. The Selçuk Turks dominated much of Anatolia, that vast steppe of Turkey between the Black and Mediterranean Seas, from the 11th to 13th centuries. Two centuries later, the Ottomans ruled from İstanbul a vast territory of conquered lands in addition to Anatolia. Both had an enormous influence on the cuisine. Their reigns and food habits were richly entwined with the practices of Islam, the religion they had encountered in Persia and ultimately embraced.

Turkish Origins in Central Asia

According to available records, the early Turkish peoples were nomads in the western region of China. Not much is known about the culinary habits of these early, wandering tribes; their diets apparently included venison and rabbit until herding replaced hunting. As herdsmen, their staples were meat, milk and milk products. Fruits, berries and vegetables were sporadic additions. Not surprisingly, these nomadic tribes grilled meat on makeshift skewers over a fire.

Food preservation was a serious problem for nomadic peoples. Some of today's food products undoubtedly derive from early attempts to prevent or retard food spoilage. The tangy and salty dried meat product known as *pastırma*, which is cured with a paste of red pepper, fenugreek seeds and garlic, appears to have its antecedent in meat practices of the central Asian Turkish horsemen. By some accounts, perhaps apocryphal, pieces of meat were cured by horse sweat and wind as they hung from the sides of the animal or while tucked under the saddle. Fermenting milk to hardier yogurt, a ubiquitous ingredient of contemporary Turkish cuisine, was widely practiced by these ancient peoples. The refreshing drink *ayran,* made by diluting yogurt with water, is also attributed to these early nomads.

The first important settlement of Turkish peoples, that of the Uygurs, occurred in the 8th century in Xingjiang Province of western China. Historians note that their diet, rich in milk and various cheeses, differed from that of the neighboring Chinese, who never developed a taste for dairy products. And, unlike the Chinese, the Uygurs apparently dined on the floor at low, round tables. Today, traces of this practice are found in rural Anatolia. The Chinese contributed to the early Turkish menu a preparation called *mantı,* which consists of small, wonton-like pieces of dough stuffed with a meat or cheese mixture. This dish is still available today and typically comes smothered in a tasty yogurt and garlic sauce. Its Italian counterpart is the more familiar ravioli.

Yogurt, a key food staple of early Turkish herdsmen, remains important today. Its popularity in the cuisine of other cultures is in large part attributable to the Turks.

These little stuffed pasta tidbits certainly must have inspired the early Turks to invent their own variations. Stuffed food, the *dolma,* is a trademark of Turkish cuisine, elaborated as stuffed fruits, vegetables, meat, fish and even offal. Alternatively, wrappers such as thin meat fillets, cabbage leaves or lengthwise slices of eggplant are rolled around a filling. These dishes are called *sarma,* meaning "wrapped." In some instances, the distinction between techniques breaks down. A stuffed grape leaf is both *sarma* and *dolma,* but is more commonly referred to as *dolma.*

The Turks in Western Asia

The Turks were driven into Arab dominions in western Asia by relentless advances of the Mongols and by a need for richer soil, fresher pastures and a better growing climate. During the 10th and 11th centuries, they began establishing their own kingdoms in western Asia. The empire of one of the strongest Turkish states, the Selçuks, stretched over most of Persia, and placed them strategically at the gateway to Anatolia.

The essence of Turkish cuisine was already well defined by this time. A general dictionary of Turkish dialects was compiled by Mahmud of Kashgar in 1073 in western China. This dictionary has been an invaluable source for food historians, providing insight into prevailing Turkish cookery. Its entries include many words describing food, its growth and its preparation.

Stuffed foods, or *dolma,* have a prominent place on Turkish menus. This food preparation style can be traced to Chinese influences around the 8th century.

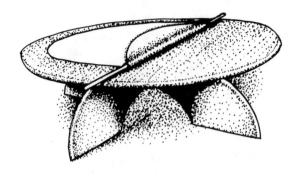

The low table, or *hamur açma sofrası,* at which Anatolian women traditionally sit and roll dough called *yufka* into thin sheets using a long, narrow rolling pin called an *oklava.*

That the Turks farmed is evident from words meaning, "to sow" and "to plow." Important crops were grains such as wheat, barley and millet. These grains formed the basis of many dishes incorporating one of several cooking methods. There was toasted grain, which was sometimes sweetened, boiled grain the consistency of mush or considerably thinner and soup-like, and grain fried in butter. The use of crushed grain, or groats, was also recorded. Noodles, breads and cakes were enjoyed, as were thin sheets of dough called *yufka,* often stacked in layers. This dough was made into savory pastries, which probably were an early form of *börek.* Cooking methods included griddle frying and baking in embers or in a *tandır,* a clay-lined pit in the ground.

The Selçuk Turks acquired several additions to their menu from the Persians. They were introduced to rice, a food unknown in central Asia. Initially made into desserts, it was used later in pilaf dishes, which the Turks continued to embellish further. In turn, the Turks taught the Persians the art of cooking with bulgur. Another Persian influence was the combination of fruits and meats in stews, and stuffings made from a mixture of nuts, currants and often rice. These influences are evident on contemporary Turkish menus. Two examples are *Acem köftesi,* which is Persian *(Acem)*-style meatballs stuffed with a mixture of pine nuts, then breaded and fried; and *Acem yahnisi,* which is a ragout of chicken with walnuts and pomegranate juice.

It was also in Persia that the Selçuk Turks encountered the religion of Islam. They converted in the 10th century, an event of considerable historical consequence, and this effectively detached them from the cultural influence of the Far East. Religion gave them an additional incentive for territorial expansion. From then on they fought holy wars in the name of Allah, trustful of the new faith that promised rewards in life and the hereafter, and the boundaries of Islam spread.

The Selçuks in Anatolia

Toward the end of the 11th century, a branch of the Selçuk dynasty in Persia advanced toward Anatolia. Under Sultan Alp Arslan, the Selçuk Turks gained control of much of Anatolia in 1071 by defeating the Christian army of Byzantine Emperor Romanos Diogenes in the battle of Malazgirt in what today is the province of Muş in Eastern Turkey. The Byzantines were forced to relinquish much of their territory, and as they withdrew, Islam rapidly spread in Anatolia.

Konya, in central Anatolia, became the political and spiritual center for the Turks, and in the 12th and 13th centuries was a renowned cultural center, attracting men of learning, mystics and poets. From the writings of religious orders and court chronicles, it is possible to trace how the cuisine of the early Islamic Turks in Anatolia evolved further.

The menu was enriched by several foods that had not been available to the Anatolian Turks before. Among the new items native to the area were cabbage, cauliflower, chickpeas, parsley and figs. The Greeks introduced them to olive oil, fish and seafood, and taught them how to bake round loaves of bread in addition to their customary flat ones.

The Selçuk sultans apparently enjoyed an epicurean cuisine. From records of a banquet given by Sultan Alâeddin Keykubad in 1237, we know he and his guests consumed kebabs of chicken and duck, a pepper-seasoned pilaf, stewed vegetables, leafy vegetables such as spinach served with a yogurt and garlic sauce, halvah and *zerde,* a saffron-flavored rice pudding.

Considerable insight into the nature of Turkish cuisine at the time is obtained from writings of the Islamic mystics (Sufis). One of the most renowned mystics and poets was Mevlânâ Celâleddin Rûmî, founder of the Mevlevî (whirling dervish) order. Members arrived at a state of ecstasy by ritual whirling to the music of flutes and drums.

Rûmî's poems record the importance of food in the life of the religious order and contain many references to the foodstuffs available in Selçuk

Anatolia. Kitchens could boast of a variety of meats, legumes, nuts, vegetables, fruits, breads, pastries, milk products, candies and pickles. The language of food typically was symbolic. Rûmî's famous poem of 26,000 couplets is laced with food imagery and symbolism. His allusions to food signified spiritual sustenance, and its processing the purification of the soul. Another poem attributed to Rûmî (mistakenly, according to some scholars) uses three simple, food-related words to summarize how a novice in the order becomes educated in the ways of Sufism until he is consumed and becomes one with God: "I was raw, I was cooked, and I was burned."

The Sufi poet Kaygusuz Abdal also specialized in using food imagery in his mystical poems. In his most well-known work he described buying and cooking a goose for 40 days, yet the goose remained raw. His metaphor is the 40 days of penance a novice undergoes before he is esteemed worthy of joining the order.

An attractive, hand-painted ceramic plate with intricate floral motif, an example of one of Turkey's flourishing traditional decorative arts.

The consumption of a particular sweet known as *helva*, or halvah, became an important part of the Sufi religious ceremony. Considered an especially luscious mortal edible, it was equated with the sweetness of spiritual rapture and was eaten at the end of the ritual where a spiritual merging with the divine was sought by repeated invocation of a holy chant.

Even the customs of ordinary, everyday events associated with serving and eating in the religious orders became a rich source of culinary information about the period. Much is known about the communities of the Mevlevî and Bektaşî dervish orders. Their kitchens were considered sacred places, with special reverence accorded the large fireplaces they contained. It was in this room that novices were educated and initiated into the brotherhood. Members were given specific duties associated with food preparation within the lodge, becoming known as pilaf maker, sherbet maker, and so forth. These positions were part of a complex hierarchy. The ranking member of the order, the chief cook, had under his supervision not only individuals responsible for making specific dishes, but those procuring ingredients, and cleaning up afterwards. Novices started with menial jobs, and were promoted within the ranks as they became spiritually more mature. At the completion of their training they were considered "cooked" and became full members of the order. Eating itself occurred under rigid rules to ensure that all ate equal portions of food.

Ottoman Turkish Cuisine

The fragmentation of the Selçuk empire in Anatolia, begun about the middle of the 13th century both by internal disorder and the Mongols, paved the way for independent Turkish bands to carve up the former Selçuk state into smaller, rival fiefdoms. The tribe of Osman, from which Ottoman derives, swept away all challengers over a period of about two centuries and ultimately snatched from the Byzantines the coveted prize of Constantinople (now İstanbul) in 1453. This new capital of the Ottoman Empire, which was called Kostantiniyye into the 20th century, was home to the sultans for the duration of their dynasty, which lasted 600 years.

Sultan Mehmet II the Conqueror wasted little time erecting the splendid Topkapı Palace in İstanbul shortly after he took over the city. Judging from the huge kitchen it housed, topped with four large domes, it was apparent that culinary arts played a major role in daily affairs. In fact, Turkish cuisine under the tutelage of the Ottoman sultans flourished at the hands of many skilled cooks anxious to prove their mettle to the court. These cooks not only had their culinary heritage to draw upon, but had access to just about every existing ingredient. The vast empire of the Ottomans grew to encompass territory north to Vienna, south to the Arabian Peninsula and west to include most of northern Africa. Products of all sorts, including foodstuffs and exotic spices, found their way to İstanbul by various land and water routes. These became a part of an ever growing repertoire of dishes that appeared in the sumptuous, multiple-course meals presented to the sultans.

All the while, the size and complexity of the kitchen staff increased to feed the growing number of people living on the palace grounds, literally a walled city, which included the royal household, the court, the government, mosques, hospitals, teachers, caretakers and the sultan's elite corps of guards known as the *Janissaries*. At the end of the 16th century, according to extensive records maintained by the palace, a staff of 200 live-in cooks toiled in the kitchen. In a mere 50 years, this number rose to about 1,400. They fed up to 10,000 people in a single day, including those meals destined for diners outside the palace as a token of the sultan's favor. To accommodate this flurry of culinary activity, the kitchen was enlarged to a structure of several buildings under 10 domes. Some years later, the kitchen underwent a doubling in size with the addition of 10 more sections.

The organization required for a culinary operation of this size to run smoothly was staggering. Every imaginable food category had not one, but an entire staff of cooks devoted to the art of preparing and perfecting it. For one dessert alone, *helva,* six versions were made, each requiring a chef and a hundred apprentices. All food personnel were part of a complex infrastructure. At the top was the *matbah emini,* the trustee of the royal kitchens. The hierarchy also included a prodigious administrative staff that oversaw the purchase, storage, preparation and serving of tons of foodstuffs arriving at the palace kitchen each year.

By the royal decree of Sultan Mehmet II the Conqueror, all civilian and military people wore outer garments and turbans of a specific style and color to facilitate recognition of their vocation and position within the hierarchy on sight. The culinary staff of the palace was not immune to this edict, and a rich variety of garments and styles characterized these jobs.

The Ottoman court provided ample opportunity for creativity in the kitchen, as many were eager to please the sultan and gain promotion. Contemporary menus offer several dishes of Ottoman origin, some with

pleasantly sensual names such as "lady's thigh," "beauty's lips" and "lady's navel." Others with interesting, descriptive names are "the priest fainted" and "his majesty liked it" (see *Menu Guide*, p. 69). Many ingenious and delicious culinary creations from the Ottoman period, however, have been nearly forgotten. Fortunately, several prominent Turkish food authorities and chefs, including Vedat Başaran at the Feriye Restaurant, located on the Bosphorus between the exquisite Dolmabahçe and Çirağan palaces in Istanbul, and the late Tuğrul Şavkay, have made a concerted effort to revive many of the sophisticated Ottoman dishes that have faded from memory.

Chief royal cook, or *hünkâr aşçıbaşısı,* in official attire. He headed the staff of cooks who prepared food for Ottoman sultans in a special palace kitchen.

The abundance of food and quality of dining outside the palace grounds was in the hands of special guilds, about 43 of them, which regulated the cost and quality of the food. At the hub of this effort was the indoor Egyptian Market, still in existence today, which housed a vast selection of foodstuffs in addition to spices and herbs, and provided for the whole city of İstanbul.

Food in the Ottoman Military

For centuries the sultans' army, the *Janissary* corps, was made up of young, Christian men recruited from captured countries who were educated into a life of Islam and fierce devotion to the sultan. Food played an important role in this elite military corps. Members were organized into divisions, each with its own barracks on the palace grounds and a huge copper cauldron, called a *kazan,* in which their pilaf was prepared. These kettles became important symbols to each unit. The loss of one during war marked the entire unit with disgrace and dismissal. It also served as a symbolic gesture to show dissatisfaction with the sultan or a high official in his court. An overturned kettle signified rebellion in the ranks, and sometimes a head rolled before order was restored.

Some of the officers in the corps held positions that bore names of food-related activities, but it is not clear they ever actually performed them. The top commanders were called soupmen. Others below them were the chief cook, scullion, pancake maker, bread baker and water carrier.

Special-Occasion Foods

The Islamic calendar has a rich association with food. Religious holidays commemorate events that are marked with the preparation of special dishes for family and friends and are also a time when particular attention is directed toward feeding the neediest.

The first significant holiday of the Muslim year actually commemorates two events said to occur on the 10th day of the first lunar month, Muharrem. It is both the day that Imam Hüseyin, grandson of the Prophet Mohammed, was martyred and the day that Noah and his family were able to leave the Ark after the flood waters receded. A thick, sweet pudding called *aşure,* or Noah's pudding, is the traditional food made this day, using the same ingredients supposedly remaining in the Ark after it was able to land. The ritual preparation of this dessert, a complex mixture of fresh and dried fruits, nuts, legumes and grains, originated in the kitchens of the Bektaşî dervish sect. With solemn pomp

A confectioner, or *helvacı,* in official attire. He cooked in the *helvahane,* the section of the palace kitchen devoted to making *helva* and other confections, including jams and jellies.

The *kazan,* or copper cauldron, used to prepare pilaf for the *Janissaries,* the sultan's army.

and prayer everyone in the sect would take a turn at stirring the concoction as it simmered in a big cauldron over the fire. The finished product would then be eaten, and much was distributed to the poor.

The ninth month, Ramazan (Ramadan), is a holy month with observances similar to Lent. For thirty days the faithful fast between sunrise and sunset in repentence for their sins of the past year. Much of the day is devoted to preparing food for *iftar,* the meal taken to break the fast. Not quite the feast it used to be, a typical menu includes samples of various cheeses, meats such as *sucuk* and *pastırma,* and a special *pide,* followed by soup and dinner. The traditional dessert of Ramazan is *güllâç,* a rose-flavored pudding made of finely ground nuts and paper-thin rice wafers soaked in milk.

Immediately following Ramazan are three days of festivities, called *Şeker Bayramı,* the Festival of Sugar, which celebrates the end of the fast. It is a happy time spent socializing and exchanging gifts of *lokum* (Turkish Delight) and other sweets.

Kurban Bayramı, the four day Festival of Sacrifice, is the last holy time of the Muslim year, beginning the 10th day of the 12th month. It commemorates the near sacrifice of Isaac by his father Abraham. God spared the child, allowing a lamb to be sacrificed instead. Throughout the country, those who can afford it sacrifice an animal in memory of this event and reserve a portion of the meat for the poor. Traditionally, some of the meat is fried in its own fat on a convex griddle, or *saç,* to make the dish called *kavurma.*

Several minor holy days called *Kandil Geceleri,* or lamp nights, are celebrated during the year. Mosques are illuminated in the evenings, and strings of lights run between minarets. A special *mahleb*-flavored, ring-shaped roll, the *kandil simidi,* which is somewhat smaller and harder than the everyday *simit* sold on the streets, is prepared for these occasions.

Coffee and Sociability

Coffee entered the world of Islam from Yemen sometime in the mid-16th century, during the reign of Sultan Süleyman the Magnificent. Its arrival brought into existence a new institution. The sociability inherent in meeting with friends to sip coffee and discuss the affairs of the day became immensely popular, bringing into being the Turkish coffee house, or *kahvehane.* It was not a smooth beginning, however. The state of euphoria that coffee produced was poorly understood. To certain clerics, this beverage was obviously an intoxicant and therefore against Islamic law. Coupled with this was the fear that the coffee house setting was likely to unleash political unrest. On more than one occasion in the course of the next century, coffee houses were prohibited, only to re-open. When these establishments finally gained acceptance and respectability, they profoundly changed society by providing a unique opportunity to gather socially outside the home.

A *cezve,* the long-handled, wide-necked pot used to brew Turkish coffee. Depicted is an example of the fine copperware handcrafted by talented artisans in Gaziantep, a city in southeastern Anatolia.

The rise of the restaurant as a place for families to dine out for pleasure is a 20th-century development. The first establishments were called *aşevi,* meaning "house of cooked food." These were followed by the *lokanta,* from the Italian word for inn. The newer, more westernized eateries were called *restoran.* More-traditional restaurants still go by the name *lokanta,* although the distinction between *lokanta* and *restoran* is frequently blurred.

The cover of an old Turkish cookbook written in Ottoman script, published in İstanbul in 1922.

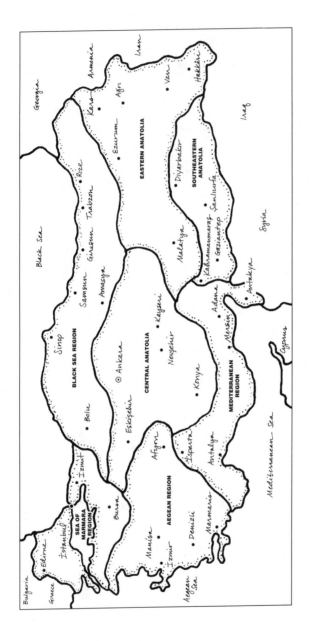

Regional Map of Turkey

Regional Turkish Food

A Quick Tour of Turkish Foods and Their Regional Variations

Turkish Food in a Nutshell

Fresh is the best first adjective to apply to Turkish cuisine. Foods are enjoyed in season. It would be unthinkable to want winter's pale and mealy tomato, coaxed to grow under greenhouse conditions. The knowledge that one of spring's earliest offerings, the tart, green soul plum, or *can eriği,* can be fully enjoyed before ripening, seems to shorten the wait for the land to turn green again.

Turkey is one of a few nations able to feed all of her people. Food is abundant and healthful, grown without chemical additives.

As a whole, Turkish cuisine is not spicy. Exceptions are found in certain parts of the southeast, where several preparations reflect a peppery Arabic influence. The most typical seasonings are mint, dill, flat-leaf parsley, paprika, cumin and *sumak,* the dried and ground berries from an edible variety of sumac shrub, which imparts a tart, lemony flavor to dishes. Usage of garlic and onions is liberal. Sauces are simple and light, with a lemon and egg yolk sauce called *terbiye,* a yogurt and garlic sauce and "au jus" predominating.

An entire meal can be made of *meze,* the infinite variety of pre-dinner tidbits on small platters, and often is. *Meze* are meant to accompany *rakı,* Turkey's anise-flavored national drink distilled from grapes. Cold dishes are followed by hot dishes and range from a simple plate of white sheep's cheese, or *beyaz peynir,* to shredded chicken in a pulverized walnut sauce and topped with paprika-flavored walnut oil, an elegant dish called *Çerkes tavuğu,* which is attributed to the Circassians.

The most popular meat appearing on the table is lamb. Beef is a distant second and pork is uncommon because it is prohibited by the Muslim religion. Poultry is also eaten. A rich family of meat dishes includes patties of seasoned minced meat called *köfte,* savory pastries of the *börek* class made with thin sheets of dough called *yufka,* and kebabs, of which the most familiar ones, *şiş kebabı,* are grilled on skewers (*şiş*).

That Turkey has a long coastline on four seas is reflected in the many varieties of fresh fish available. Much of the day's catch ends up on the grill. However, cooking procedures run the gamut from fish baked in paper to fish cakes, a type of *köfte.* Interestingly, the Turks market fish by age, naming young and old specimens differently. For example, if one wants young red mullet, one orders *tekir;* older specimens are called *barbunya.* Fried mussels are a perennial favorite in the seafood category, and are especially tasty with *tarator,* a ground nut sauce containing garlic and vinegar or lemon juice.

Vegetables are widely enjoyed by the Turks and eggplant is number one. Note that the Turkish eggplant is a richer-flavored, longer, thinner variety than the type commonly available in the United States. A classic preparation, *imam bayıldı,* or "the priest fainted," is a cold dish of eggplant stuffed with chopped tomatoes, onions, garlic and parsley, then stewed in olive oil. It is also an example of *dolma,* or stuffed food, although the *dolma*

Asma yaprağında sardalya, or sardines wrapped in grape leaves, is grilled over charcoal and garnished with lemon slices to create a popular main course.

tradionally contains a rice stuffing, with or without meat. Only *dolma* with meat, however, are served hot, typically with yogurt sauce. Other popular vegetables are tomatoes, peppers, squash and fresh green beans, to name just a few.

Fruit lovers will think they are in paradise. Strawberries, peaches, figs, melons, cherries, apricots, grapes, quinces—an endless list—are plentiful and are eaten primarily fresh, stuffed or in two types of cold compote. *Hoşaf* is a compote made with small fruits such as grapes and apricots, usually dried, which are stewed in sugar and water or in *pekmez,* a molasses made from grape juice. When large fresh fruits such as peaches or pears are used, the dish is known as *komposto.*

Warm, soothing soups are ubiquitous menu items. Lentils (red or green) and an assortment of other vegetables are favorite ingredients. An interesting soup, *tarhana çorbası,* is made from a soup base called *tarhana,* consisting of of flour, yeast, tomatoes and red peppers. It is fermented, dried, pulverized and stored at room temperature until needed for making soup. One of the most traditional offerings is *işkembe çorbası,* or tripe soup, which is believed to ward off hangovers. For this reason, special restaurants, called *işkembeci,* are often open all night!

Pilafs showcase rice. Recipes have to be followed carefully to ensure that individual rice grains do not stick together. Among the caveats is that one refrains from stirring the rice while it is cooking, and stirs afterwards only with a wooden spoon to prevent the grains from breaking. So exacting is this art that aspiring chefs often are hired on the basis of this skill. A variety of ingredients such as nuts, raisins, tomatoes, onions, currants, even liver can be added to embellish one. Pilafs also are made of bulgur.

Breads show a rich versatility. The mainstay are crusty, aromatic loaves. *Pide,* a delicious flat bread, appears in many guises, including as the base for various toppings that transform it into a pizza-like dish. Twisted, ring-shaped rolls, or *simit,* encrusted with sesame seeds, are the most popular street food.

The dessert category bursts with temptations, but most sweets are enjoyed with tea, not following meals. Fruit is the typical end to dinner. One of the most inventive Turkish desserts belongs to the milk-based pudding family. It is *tavuk göğsü,* a rice flour pudding containing finely shredded chicken breast. So smooth is this pudding that it is nigh impossible for the unknowing to detect this unexpected ingredient. Huge trays of *baklava* and other, lesser-known pastry confections made from *yufka* beckon the sweet tooth, as do similar preparations made of fine threads of dough called *tel kadayıf.*

Rich, thick cream called *kaymak,* once traditionally made with buffalo milk, is served with some of these treats. Countless others await discovery by the traveler.

Coffee and tea are both Turkish institutions, but most Turks crave tea after dining. In fact, they drink tea all day long, during business negotiations or socializing. Tea is a brisk business. Little glasses of tea, carefully balanced on trays suspended by three metal chains, are borne by boys scurrying up and down the streets, waiting for the nod to bring another round. It is said that tea is served in glasses so that the important qualities of clarity and color can be more clearly ascertained. Precisely two cubes of sugar appear on every saucer.

Those who travel long distances by car or bus in Turkey are immediately impressed at the great diversity in the landscape. In a matter of a few hours, one can experience verdant farmlands, forests and arid plains. Mountain ranges appear and disappear with remarkable regularity. In this land of contrasting environments, it is not surpising to find many regional culinary variations. Some of these specialties, however, will only be found by looking farther than the usual tourist dining spots, where more and more western

Countless tea gardens attest to the national pastime of drinking tea. Served in delicate, tulip-shaped glasses, tea is a unifying element among the varied social and regional aspects of Turkish culture.

offerings crowd out the tradional dishes. Lucky travelers may even be presented the opportunity to dine in a home to experience regional cuisine in its most authentic setting.

The Sea of Marmara Region

The Sea of Marmara region includes the area of Turkey in Europe called Thrace and the land surrounding the Sea of Marmara, reaching to the western shore of the Black Sea and to the northern shore of the Aegean. This is an important fruit- and vegetable-growing region. Olive groves and sunflower fields dot the rolling hills. A strong Greek heritage is evident here.

The Dardanelles and the Bosphorus separate European and Asian Turkey. Along the shores of the latter, on two continents, sits the former capital, İstanbul, city of many splendors and the culinary center of the country. Whatever is desired can be found in this city of myriad delights. The vibrant Egyptian Market, or *Mısır Çarşısı,* still the place to find purveyors of exotic spices and a plethora of other foodstuffs, is a first destination for food enthusiasts. For nonedibles, the gigantic Covered Bazaar, or *Kapalı Çarşı,* is the awesome commercial center of the old city. Four thousand shops and a few restaurants tempt the shopper in its labyrinthine passageways.

Many districts of İstanbul have become recognized over the years for specific culinary specialities. To name just a few, Kanlıca is famous for its creamy yogurt literally thick enough to slice. *Kanlıca yoğurdu* is served by the slice, with powdered sugar on the side. Beykoz is known for its style of cooking sheep's trotters. This preparation, called *Beykoz usülü paça,* comes cooked in garlic and olive oil, served on a slice of fried bread, topped with a lemon and egg yolk sauce called *terbiye.*

İstanbul has long been a fisherman's paradise. In the past, fishermen constructed offshore scaffolding, or *dalyan,* and posted a sentinel atop it to sight schools of fish. When their quarry came close enough, a stone was hurled into the water, and if well-placed, would cause fish to swim toward nets and be trapped. A favorite fish then and today is mackerel, although the modern scourge of pollution has taken its toll on the catch. It is used in one of İstanbul's classic and delicious appetizers, *uskumru dolması,* or stuffed mackerel. The preparation of this dish is not for the dilettante. Bone and flesh have to be arduously removed without cutting the skin, which is then restuffed with a mixture made of the flesh, rice, pine nuts and currants. It is then breaded and deep-fried. The most beloved fish of an İstanbullu, however, is the *lüfer,* a fish similar to the bluefish, which is indigenous to the Bosphorus. They are attracted to light and are still fished in the evening by lamplight, quite a romantic sight from shore. It will be helpful to know that *çinakop* is a small, young *lüfer. Koruk lüferi* and *sarı kanat* refer to medium-size fish; *kofana* is a large specimen. A popular local dish is *çinakop ızgara,* or grilled (young) *lüfer.*

One of the sinful desserts originating in İstanbul is *kazan dibi,* which means "bottom of the kettle." Historically, this dessert was the somewhat

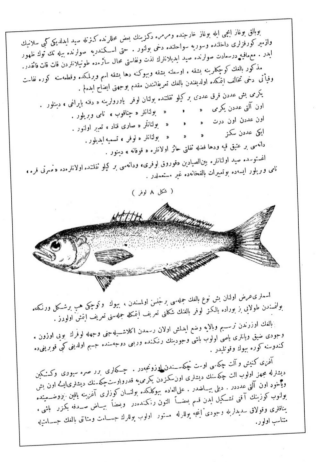

A page from an old fishing treatise written in Ottoman script. Depicted is the highly regarded *lüfer,* unique to the Bosphorus, whose delicate white flesh typically is grilled.

burned remnants stuck to the bottom of the pot when making another famous pudding called *tavuk göğsü*. It is a firm, milk and rice flour pudding, rolled like a jelly roll, with a dark brown surface obtained by letting the bottom of the pudding brown over a burner.

While it is possible in İstanbul to sample the infinite variety of regional Turkish specialities, it is quite pleasing to enjoy them in their natural setting. The early capitals of the Ottoman Empire, Bursa and Edirne, are within the Marmara area. Bursa is home of the *Bursa kebabı,* a kebab made with thin slices of lamb cut from a large, wedge-shaped slab of meat (itself the classic *döner kebabı),* which is roasted on an upright, slowly revolving spit. For the Bursa-style kebab, slices of meat are placed on top of fresh *pide* bread after it has been spread with tomato sauce and covered with whipped yogurt. Browned butter is then drizzled over everything. Another name for this specialty is *İskender kebabı,* after a famous kebab restaurant in Bursa. The area around Bursa is famous for its peaches and chestnuts. A regional specialty is the sweet called *kestane şekeri,* or chestnut glacé. Edirne is known for its fine *kaşar peyniri,* a mild, yellow cheese made from sheep's milk. The local treat in İzmit is *pişmaniye,* a white, spun-sugar confection similar to cotton candy. Another regional dish, *İnegöl köftesi,* is grilled meatballs containing semolina.

The Aegean

The Aegean is a rich agricultural region encompassing miles of coastline as far south as Fethiye and an area inland, or eastward, about two hundred miles including the cities of Afyon, Denizli and Muğla. The terrain is studded with olive groves, vineyards, orchards and cultivated fields. Figs, grapes, olives, oranges, lemons, tangerines and a variety of vegetables grow in abundance.

Not surprisingly, olive oil is a staple of the region. The method of stewing vegetables in olive oil, or *zeytinyağlı,* is very popular here. These preparations are always served cold (room temperature) and many different vegetables, both stuffed and unstuffed, are fixed in this manner. Classics are *zeytinyağlı yaprak dolması,* or stuffed vine leaves in olive oil, and *zeytinağlı patlıcan dolması,* or stuffed eggplant in olive oil. Even stuffed squash blossoms are enjoyed this way.

21

The Hellem Nooh, one of many yachts for hire plying the waters of the Aegean and Mediterranean Seas. Cooking aficionados can take over its galley and get first-hand experience cooking Turkish cuisine, after shopping the local market for fresh produce.

A dish traditionally prepared in the Aegean region is the soup called *oğmaç çorbası,* or rubbed noodle soup. Small pieces of cooked pasta, formed by rubbing together a mixture of flour, salt and egg, are added to a yogurt-based soup flavored with parsley. Sometimes tomato or mint is also included.

Turkey's third largest city, İzmir, is in the Aegean region. Peaches, chestnuts, almonds, figs and grapes grow in the surrounding countryside. Dried figs and sultanas (raisins) raised near İzmir are highly prized. A popular local treat is *incir dolması,* or stewed figs, stuffed with a sweetened nut mixture. Acclaimed fish of the area are *trança,* or halibut, and *çipura,* a flat fish resembling pompano. This region's version of *köfte,* called *İzmir köftesi,* consists of sausage-shaped pieces of a cumin-flavored, minced lamb mixture topped with tomato sauce and cooked green bell peppers.

A specialty of Afyon is *kaymak,* a thick, rich cream traditionally made from buffalo milk. It is reduced by boiling until firm enough to slice, and is used as a dessert filling or accompaniment. The taste treat to savor in Afyon is *ekmek kadayıfı,* made from special bread dough presoaked in hot water to soften and swell it, and then baked in sugar syrup. Pieces are split and filled with *kaymak,* or simply topped with a generous dollop of it. This cream neutralizes the excessive sweetness of the dessert. Other local dishes are *mercimekli bükme böreği,* a *börek* filled with lentils, and *haşhaşlı nokul,* or poppy seed rolls using seeds from Afyon-grown poppies.

The coastal town of Marmaris is known for the varieties of honey produced in the area. *Çam balı,* a dark, pine-scented honey, is most popular.

The Mediterranean

The Mediterranean region includes the southern coast of Turkey from Fethiye extending eastward to the Bay of İskenderun. The principal coastal resort is the city of Antalya. An inland area up to about one hundred miles is

A tea samovar. Tea leaves in the teapot on top steep to make a strong infusion, which is diluted "to taste" with hot water in the samovar.

also a part of this region. It includes what is known as the Lake District near Isparta and the cities of Adana, Mersin and Antakya. The rich soil supports olive and citrus groves, and banana and avocado plantations. The crops of laurel (bay) leaves and oregano are also important.

A classic soup of the area is *yüksük çorbası,* or thimble soup. It contains ground meat, chickpeas and small, thin circles of dough, traditionally cut out with a thimble. Surrounding Isparta in the Lake District are large rose gardens producing oils used in the perfume industry. An edible by-product of this effort is delicious rose-flavored jam. Jams and preserves made from locally grown fruits are a specialty of Antalya, as are several cold *meze,* or appetizers. *Hibeş* is a paste made of yogurt, chickpeas, red pepper and onion, which is spread on *pide* bread. *Şakşuka* is a mixture of chopped eggplant, tomato and green pepper. Another is *cevizli tulum peyniri,* which is made with walnuts mixed with *tulum peyniri,* an aged, salty cheese. A cold bean salad in vinaigrette, called *piyaz,* is also representative of the area.

The eastern portion of the Mediterranean region has had a strong Arabic influence, reflected in the peppery nature of many dishes. In Mersin, a classic soup is *Arabaşı çorbası,* or Arab's soup, a nippy tomato and chicken soup with hot red pepper paste. Sometimes cold cubes of a cooked batter

Heavy ceramic lids used as weights on top of vegetable preparations called *sarma*. These lids keep leafy wrappings from unfolding and spilling their contents during cooking.

of flour and water are put in the soup to complement its spiciness and temperature. Another local dish is *sarımsaklı köfte,* or balls of steamed bulgur in a tomato, garlic and red pepper sauce. The food of Adana can also be hot. A celebrated specialty is *Adana kebabı.* These are spicy, flattened sausage-shaped kebabs of minced lamb, which are grilled on broad, flat skewers. They are served on pieces of *pide* bread and garnished with roasted tomatoes and peppers. A relish of thinly sliced onions, flat-leaf parsley and *sumak* typically accompanies this dish. As in other preparations with raw onions, the Turks cleverly minimize the burning sensation and strong smell of the onions by first rubbing them with salt and then washing away the salt with water. A local soup is *Adana çorbası,* which contains tiny meatballs, chickpeas and tomatoes, flavored with a touch of vinegar.

Some of the traditional dishes of Antakya feature bulgur. *Ekşi aşı* is a piquant, yogurt-based soup with rice, chickpeas, herbs and small, sausage-shaped pieces of minced meat coated with bulgur. *Oruk* is a dish made with oblong, tapered balls of bulgur, poked with a finger to make an opening, and filled with a mixture of minced lamb, walnuts, flat-leaf parsley, onions and cumin. A typical appetizer is *cevizli biber,* a paste of ground walnuts, mashed red bell peppers and onions, spiked with hot red pepper to taste. Also regional is the paste called *muhammara,* which is of Arabic origin. It consists of ground walnuts, roasted red bell peppers, bread crumbs, hot red pepper and garlic, mixed with olive oil and seasoned with pomegranate syrup.

Central Anatolia

Central Anatolia is the heartland, the breadbasket of Turkey. Wheat fields stretch endlessly across the rolling steppes. It is also a land of fruits, vegetables and livestock pasturage. Ankara, the capital of Turkey since 1923, is located here as are the cities of Konya, Eskişehir and Sivas. Cappadocia, an area with bizarre formations carved out of volcanic ash by wind erosion, is the site of the cities of Nevşehir, Kayseri and Ürgüp.

Specialties of the area include *böreks* traditionally baked in a *tandır,* a clay-lined pit or oven. *Kıymalı tandır böreği* has a filling of ground meat. *Kabak böreği* has a filling of zucchini. Also representative of the region are *gözleme,* thin circles of rolled dough covered with meat, cheese or vegetables and folded like an envelope before being fried on an inverted griddle called a *saç*. A round, flat bread, called *bazlama,* is also grilled on the *saç*.

Several dishes are associated with Konya. *Fırın kebabı* is roast mutton. Generous, tender hunks of it are served with fresh *pide* bread. Another local dish is *etli pide,* also called *etli ekmek,* or bread with meat. It is a pizza-like preparation made with thin *pide* bread covered with minced lamb, three varieties of grated cheese *(kaşar, tulum and beyaz peynir)* and green pepper. *Saç arası* is a scrumptious, syrup-soaked dessert made of *yufka* topped with crushed pistachios.

In Cappadocia, the city of Kayseri is known for *Kayseri köftesi,* cumin-flavored, minced meat patties covered with sliced tomatoes, which are baked on top of sliced potatoes. Another local preparation is *pastırma böreği,* a *börek* made with *pastırma,* dried and salted meat cured with a paste of red pepper, fenugreek seeds and garlic. Dishes associated with Ürgüp are *kiremit kebabı,* minced lamb patties cooked on a clay tile, and *çömlek kababı*. This lamb and vegetable dish is baked in an earthenware pot traditionally made in nearby Avanos, a city famous for pottery making. A local sweet of Nevşehir is *pekmezli ayva dolması,* or stuffed quince with *pekmez,* a molasses made from grape juice.

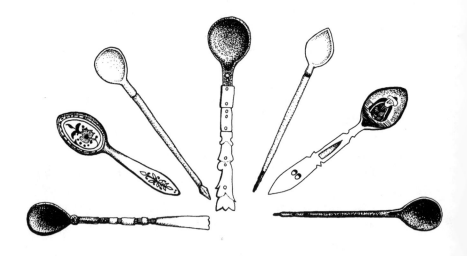

An assortment of spoons, the traditional eating utensil of Turkey. Those of the poor were typically made of wood. The urban rich had a variety of materials to choose from, including ivory and tortoise shell. Painted wooden spoons are popular souvenir items.

The Black Sea Region

The Black Sea region, especially to the east, has the benefit of generous rainfall and is blessed with rich vegetation. The warm, wet climate favors the growth of corn, hazelnuts, tea, cherries and tobacco. Corn flour is used extensively in this part of Turkey. The region also produces large crops of apples, pears, walnuts, mulberries, plums, apricots and *kara lâhana,* a black-leaf cabbage. Much of the fruit becomes *pestil,* dried sheets of fruit pulp rolled like jelly rolls.

Prominent coastal cities include Sinop, Samsun, Giresun, Trabzon and Rize. The important crop of tea is grown just east of Rize, on the steep hillside slopes reaching to the sea. The Turkish people of this eastern-most stretch of the Black Sea, the Lâz, show strong evidence of their Pontic Greek past. In addition to growing tea, hazelnuts and tobacco, they earn their livelihood as fishermen, netting an anchovy-like fish, the *hamsi,* which is the mainstay of their diet. Eaten fresh, these beloved fish are prepared many ways. A particularly elegant pilaf, *hamsili pilâv,* is made by covering black pepper-flavored rice pilaf with a layer of butterflied fish and then baking the preparation. Not unexpectedly, *hamsi* is used in regional versions of the *börek, köfte* and *dolma. Hamsi köftesi* is a fried patty of ground fish coated with cornmeal. The *dolma* is called *hamsi kuşu* because of its resemblance to a bird *(kuş):* two butterflied fish surrounding a filling of rice are coated with cornmeal and fried.

A wealth of poems, stories, songs and folk dances are based on the importance of *hamsi* to the Lâz people. For example, there is a fried fish preparation, *hamsi tavası,* which has inspired a popular song beginning "I put the *hamsi* in the skillet and started to dance!" Folk dances of the region have rapid and sharp movements, and some say they depict the swimming pattern of the fish.

Other local dishes of the Black Sea's eastern coastal region include the soup *kara lâhana çorbası,* made with black cabbage leaves, and *etli kara lâhana sarma,* a minced meat mixture wrapped in black cabbage leaves. A delectable dessert is *Lâz böreği,* made with *yufka* filled with rice pudding, subtly flavored with black pepper. A noted dish from the Trabzon area is *Trabzon kızartması,* an appetizer of deep-fried eggplant in a garlic and yogurt sauce.

Inland cities of the Black Sea region include Bolu, Safranbolu, Amasya and Gümüşhane. Bolu is the traditional home of Turkey's master chefs, who

Traditional items of the kitchen: a ewer for pouring water, a pepper grinder and a delicately hand-painted ceramic plate.

receive their training at the nearby chef's school in Mengen. Safranbolu is known for the saffron fields nearby and the quality of its *lokum,* or Turkish delight, a type of candy made with cornstarch, syrup, flavoring and various other ingredients such as nuts and dried fruits. A rich pastry filled with walnuts, called *cevizli çörek,* is representative of Amasya.

Eastern Anatolia

Eastern Anatolia is typically mountainous with high plateaus. Much of the land is pastoral. Areas under cultivation are surrounded by whole stretches of bleak, arid steppe; winters are cold and summers cool. Erzurum, on a high plateau, is the largest city in eastern Anatolia. A large Kurdish population is found in this region.

Meat, yogurt, cheeses, grains and honey are typical foods here. Both Van and Kars are known for honey. A local specialty of Van is *tutmaç,* also known as *tutmaç aşı,* a green lentil soup with homemade noodles. Elazığ, a farming community, is a grape-growing region. One of its specialities is *Harput köftesi,* balls of minced meat and bulgur in tomato sauce.

Malatya, a rich agricultural center, is the apricot capital of Turkey and also produces an excellent crop of cherries. This city is especially known for its *dolma,* because they are prepared with so many different types of leaves. One of the local favorites is *Malatya usülü fasulye yaprağı dolması.* This "Malatya style" dish has green bean leaves wrapped around a stuffing of hulled wheat and bulgur, simmered in yogurt sauce and topped with sautéed onions.

Yogurt soup, *yoğurt çorbası,* is a traditional offering of the region. Other specialties include *kete,* a flaky pastry filled with browned flour, and *aksan,* a cold salad of potatoes flavored with mint and basil, and garnished with black olives. A regional version of *köfte* from the province of Bitlis is *Bitlis köftesi,* balls of minced lamb and bulgur stuffed with a mixture of rice and pomegranate seeds.

Southeastern Anatolia

The southeastern region of Turkey is primarily hot and dry, but more arable land is being created by government irrigation projects. The often peppery cuisine of the region shows a strong Arabic influence. Some of the key cities in the region are Diyarbakır, Gaziantep, Şanlıurfa and Kahramanmaraş. This area also has a large Kurdish population.

Diyarbakır's culinary fame derives from its delicious melons. Gaziantep, formerly Antep, is the pistachio capital of the country. Luscious dessert treats, especially of the baklava family, contain copious amounts of the tasty nutmeats. Nearby Şanlıurfa provides sheep's butter of almost legendary quality and flavor to make these desserts. Another spectacular treat is *künefe,* made with fine strands of pastry dough called *tel kadayıf.* Fresh cheese is placed between two layers of butter-soaked pastry. It is baked, then drenched in syrup, sprinkled with chopped pistachio nuts and served piping hot.

The city of Gaziantep is on few itineraries, so its varied and exciting regional menu is practically undiscovered by travelers. One exceptional dish is *yuvarlama,* a preparation of small meat and bulgur balls in a spicy tomato sauce, given a piquant taste by the addition of unripe plum paste. It also has flour and water dough balls that are slightly larger than chickpeas. *İçli köfte* are oblong, tapered patties of minced lamb and bulgur, poked with a finger to make an opening, and filled with a minced meat, spice and pistachio nut mixture, sometimes containing rice. They can be boiled or fried. A simpler preparation of this dish is called *sini köftesi*. The ingredients are the same but the mixture is baked in a dish, with two layers of meat mixture separated by a filling of minced lamb, walnuts and pistachios. *Ali Nazik kebabı,* a purée of roasted eggplant, mixed with yogurt and topped with seasoned, minced lamb, is a local version of the famous Ottoman dish *hünkâr beğendi.* The popular street food is *lahmacun,* a soft, thin dough lightly spread with a spicy paste of minced lamb, tomatoes, green peppers, garlic, onion and hot red pepper.

A specialty of Şanlıurfa, formerly Urfa, is *Urfa kebabı,* long, sausage-shaped pieces of minced lamb grilled on a skewer and served on top of toasted pieces of *pide* bread that have been softened with broth.

Kahramanmaraş, formerly Maraş, is justly celebrated for its fantastic "elastic" ice cream. Powdered orchid root, or *sahleb,* an additive that thickens and flavors the ice cream, produces the taffy-like consistency. This unique treat is sold throughout Turkey by colorfully costumed vendors, who delight in showcasing the remarkable qualities of their product. The city is also known for the dish *külbastı,* grilled lamb cutlets with *çemen,* a paste made primarily of red pepper, fenugreek seeds and garlic.

The *güğüm,* a lidded copper pot with a handle and small pouring spout. By tradition, it was kept on the stove so a supply of warm water would always be available for washing hands.

Tastes of Turkey

You are encouraged to try some of these classic Turkish recipes before you leave home. This is a wonderful and immediately rewarding way to preview the extraordinary cuisine of Turkey. Most of the special Turkish ingredients necessary for these recipes are available in the United States (see *Resources,* p. 57). Satisfactory substitutes are given for unavailable ones.

May we suggest that you begin your meal in the Turkish tradition by sampling several delicious appetizers (*meze*) while sipping *rakı,* Turkey's national drink, distilled from grapes and flavored with anise. Appetizers should contrast in taste, texture and color; cold ones are served before hot ones. *Rakı,* when diluted with ice cubes or water before drinking, changes from clear to milky white. Some believe the effect of the alcohol is counteracted by drinking at the same time a concoction of beet and carrot juice flavored with lemon, called *şalgam.*

If you like to drink wine with your meal, try some imported Turkish wine. Those outside large metropolitan areas, however, may find it difficult to locate some. Turkish wines are not extensively distributed in the United States. Two, more accessible brands are Kavaklıdere and Doluca. For mail-order suppliers of Turkish wines and spirits, see *Resources (p. 57).*

APPETIZERS

Mercimek Köftesi

Lentil balls. Serves 12.

The recipe for this appetizer was provided by İstanbul native Gülseren Ramazanoğlu, author of *Turkish Cooking.*

> 2 CUPS RED LENTILS
>
> 6 CUPS WATER
>
> SALT TO TASTE
>
> 3 CUPS BULGUR,* FINELY GROUND

31

[Mercimek köftesi, *continued*]

> 1 LARGE ONION, FINELY CHOPPED
>
> 4 LARGE SCALLIONS, FINELY CHOPPED
>
> 4 LONG, THIN GREEN PEPPERS, VERY THINLY SLICED
>
> 1 CUP LOOSELY PACKED FLAT-LEAF PARSLEY, FINELY CHOPPED
>
> 2 TABLESPOONS TOMATO PASTE
>
> 2 TABLESPOONS PAPRIKA PASTE
>
> 1 TEASPOON ALLSPICE
>
> BLACK PEPPER TO TASTE
>
> 3 TABLESPOONS BUTTER OR MARGARINE

Wash lentils. Bring to boil in salted water. Lower heat and simmer about 30 minutes until lentils are very tender (like a purée) and have absorbed most of the water. Stir in bulgur and half of the onions. Remove from heat. Allow to cool. Drain. Make a hole in the middle of the lentil mixture and combine scallions, pepperones, parsley, tomato paste, paprika paste, allspice and black pepper, reserving a small amount of parsley for garnish. Knead. Sauté remaining onion in butter and add to the mixture. Knead again. Form walnut-size balls and flatten them a little. Transfer to a serving platter. Sprinkle with remaining parsley. Serve at room temperature.

*Be sure to use bulgur, not cracked wheat.

Kısır

Bulgur salad. Serves 4.

This recipe was provided by Vedat Başaran, executive chef and manager of the luxurious Feriye restaurant along the Bosphorus in İstanbul. This appetizer traditionally is offered before tea on special occasions such as the monthly open houses when Turkish women receive guests.

> 1 CUP BULGUR,* FINELY GROUND
>
> ⅔ CUP BOILING WATER
>
> 1 LARGE ONION, FINELY CHOPPED
>
> 3 LARGE TOMATOES, PEELED, SEEDED AND CHOPPED
>
> 1 CUP LOOSELY PACKED FLAT-LEAF PARSLEY, FINELY CHOPPED
>
> 3 TABLESPOONS OLIVE OIL
>
> 2 TEASPOONS RED PEPPER FLAKES†
>
> ½ TEASPOON SALT
>
> 1 TABLESPOON POMEGRANATE JUICE (OR 2 TABLESPOONS LEMON JUICE)††

SALAD GREENS OR BOILED GRAPE LEAVES

TOMATO SLICES

PICKLES

Put the bulgur in a bowl and stir in the water, a few spoonfuls at a time. Cover and let rest for 15 minutes at room temperature. Add onion to bulgur and combine thoroughly. Then stir in the other ingredients, seasoning to taste. Line a serving dish with salad greens or boiled vine leaves and top with the bulgur mixture. Garnish with sliced tomatoes or pickles. Serve at room temperature.

*Be sure to use bulgur, not cracked wheat.

†See *Resources* (p. 57) for mail-order suppliers.

††Can substitute pomegranate syrup, diluted 1 tablespoon to 1 cup water. See *Resources* (p. 57) for mail-order suppliers.

Muhammara

A spread of roasted red peppers, ground walnuts, hot pepper paste and garlic with pomegranate syrup. Serves 8.

The recipe for this appetizer was provided by Deniz Balgamış, a graduate of the University of Wisconsin, from İskenderun, a city on the eastern Mediterranean coast of Turkey.

2 LARGE RED BELL PEPPERS

1 CLOVE GARLIC, MINCED

1 SMALL ONION, FINELY CHOPPED

2 TABLESPOONS HOT PEPPER PASTE*

¾ CUP BREAD CRUMBS, TOASTED

¾ CUP WALNUTS, GROUND

3 TABLESPOONS LEMON JUICE

2 TEASPOONS POMEGRANATE SYRUP

1 TABLESPOON YOGURT

1–2 TEASPOONS CUMIN SEEDS, COARSELY GROUND

SALT TO TASTE

¼ CUP OLIVE OIL

TURKISH FLAT BREAD, OR *PIDE*†

Roast peppers over a flame until the skin is blackened. Put in a tightly closed paper bag for 10 minutes. Then remove the skin and seeds, and mash the peppers in a food processor. Set aside. Mix together the garlic, onion, hot pepper paste, bread

[Muhammara, *continued*]

crumbs and walnuts. Add peppers. When well mixed, add the lemon juice and pomegranate syrup. Add the yogurt and cumin, and salt to taste. Slowly add the olive oil and blend well. For a richer flavor, make a day ahead. Keeps well for up to 2 days in the refrigerator. Serve at room temperature on pieces of Turkish flat bread, *pide,* or plain crackers.

*See *Resources* (p. 57) for mail-order suppliers. Can substitute with a jalapeño pepper, seeded and finely chopped, or ⅛–¼ teaspoon cayenne pepper.

†See *Resources* (p. 57) for mail-order suppliers.

Uskumru Dolması

Stuffed mackerel. Serves 10.

The preparation of this elaborate appetizer involves skillfully removing the flesh and internal organs of the fish and then returning the extracted flesh, in the form of a stuffing, into the body cavity, all without a single cut or rip in the skin or removal of the head! The recipe was provided by Irvin C. Schick, a native of İstanbul, who lives in Massachusetts.

4 POUNDS FRESH, WHOLE MACKEREL, UNCLEANED*

2 MEDIUM ONIONS, FINELY CHOPPED

⅓ CUP OLIVE OIL

½ CUP WALNUTS, FINELY CHOPPED BUT NOT PULVERIZED

¼ CUP PINE NUTS

¼ CUP CURRANTS

1 BUNCH FRESH DILL, FINELY CHOPPED

1 BUNCH FRESH, FLAT-LEAF PARSLEY, FINELY CHOPPED

1 TEASPOON CINNAMON

1 TEASPOON ALLSPICE

1 TEASPOON BLACK PEPPER

SALT TO TASTE

FLOUR

BREAD CRUMBS, UNFLAVORED

4 EGGS

SAFFLOWER OR OLIVE OIL FOR DEEP-FRYING

LETTUCE LEAVES

1 LEMON, SLICED

Prepare fish for stuffing. Since it takes a while to empty each fish, keep the unprocessed fish, the extracted flesh and the fish skins refrigerated or on ice. Carefully remove the internal organs and roe through the gills and mouth and discard. Be aware of the sharp teeth and do not tear the skin. Wash fish thoroughly and drain. To remove the flesh, lay the fish on a flat surface and repeatedly pummel it on both sides with the side of the hand, like a vigorous back rub, until it feels noticeably softer. Mackerel have a tough skin, but be careful not to break it. Then bend the tail back and forth several times until the backbone snaps. Do the same just below the head. Since the fish is much thicker here, it may be easier to insert a pair of scissors through the gills or mouth and cut the backbone just behind the head. Then, with similar pummeling action, slowly massage the flesh forward and out the gills or mouth. When the flesh is loose enough, grab the backbone through the gills or mouth and pull it and any remaining attached meat out of the fish. Also watch out for other sharp bones. If the skin should tear during handling, it can be sewn afterwards, but the result won't be as pretty. Wash and drain the fish skin.

To make the stuffing, sauté the onions in olive oil until golden. Add the fish meat after carefully removing any remaining bones. Stir well so it cooks evenly and does not stick to the bottom of the pan. Add the walnuts, pine nuts, currants, herbs and spices. Continue stirring until the fish is done. The meat of the fish will turn whitish as it cooks. Stuff this mixture back into the fish through the gills or mouth. The fish should be full, but not too tightly packed or it could burst when deep-fried.

To bread the fish, place the flour and bread crumbs in two large, flat plates. Beat the eggs in a wide dish. Then take each fish and uniformly coat both sides with flour, then egg and finally bread crumbs. Heat the oil in a frying pan large enough for the fish to lie flat in it. When the oil is hot, deep-fry the fish until golden. Do not let coating that falls off and burns adhere to the fish. A rack at the bottom of the pan will help eliminate this problem. If too much coating falls off, you may have to change or strain the oil. Place the fried fish on towel paper to absorb as much oil as possible.

Serve at room temperature on a bed of lettuce with lemon slices. Cut into 1-inch slices at the table. It is best eaten the same day it is prepared or the breading will get soggy and the stuffing will be less airy.

*For easier manipulation, select short, fat fish. Do not substitute the much longer and thinner Spanish mackerel.

Haydari

A spread made with yogurt and sheep's cheese, flavored with mint and sweet-hot paprika, and drizzled with olive oil. Serves 8.

This recipe was provided by Holly Chase, author of *Turkish Tapestries: A Traveller's Portrait of Turkey.*

> 2 CUPS PLAIN YOGURT (ANY TYPE WITHOUT GELATIN ADDED)
>
> 1 TABLESPOON FINELY PULVERIZED DRIED MINT (TASTE FOR FRESH FLAVOR)

[Haydari, *continued*]

> 2 TEASPOONS SWEET-HOT PAPRIKA
>
> 4 OUNCES FLAVORFUL SHEEP'S MILK CHEESE, CRUMBLED
>
> SALT TO TASTE
>
> 2–3 TABLESPOONS FRUITY OLIVE OIL
>
> OIL-CURED BLACK OLIVES FOR DECORATION
>
> CUCUMBER SPEARS
>
> BREAD

Drain the yogurt in a cloth-lined sieve for at least 30 minutes. Add the mint and paprika to the yogurt and beat until smooth. Gently stir in the crumbled cheese to retain its texture. Chill at least 2 hours (and up to 3 days) before serving. Add salt before serving, if necessary, depending on the saltiness of the cheese used. To serve, spread the paste on a plate to a depth of ¾ inch. With the back of a spoon, make decorative indentations in the surface. Drizzle oil over the top and garnish with olives. Serve with cucumber spears and a good, crusty bread.

Sirkeli Patlıcan

Eggplant with vinegar. Serves 6.

The recipe for this appetizer was contributed by Engin E. Kadaster from İzmir, who heads Newport International Travel in Newport Beach, California.

> 1 LARGE EGGPLANT (ABOUT 1 POUND)
>
> OLIVE OR SALAD OIL FOR FRYING
>
> 4–5 CLOVES GARLIC, CHOPPED
>
> 3–4 TABLESPOONS VINEGAR
>
> SALT AND PEPPER TO TASTE
>
> A FEW SPRIGS FLAT-LEAF PARSLEY
>
> 1 MEDIUM TOMATO, SLICED (OPTIONAL)
>
> TURKISH FLAT BREAD, OR *PIDE**

Peel and cut eggplant in ¼ inch cubes. Soak in salted water for about 20 minutes, wash and dry. Heat oil in frying pan and fry eggplant cubes until golden brown. Drain and place in a serving platter. Sprinkle with chopped garlic and vinegar and mix well with a spoon. Season with salt and pepper to taste. Decorate edges with parsley and tomato slices. Place toothpicks in the eggplant cubes and serve with Turkish flat bread, *pide,* or crackers.

*See *Resources* (p. 57) for mail-order suppliers.

VEGETABLES COOKED IN OLIVE OIL

Zetinyağlı Patlıcan Dolması

Stuffed eggplant cooked in olive oil. Serves 5.

This recipe was provided by the late Tuğrul Şavkay, one of Turkey's leading food authorities, who was from Nazilli, a city on the Aegean coast.

5 LONG, THIN EGGPLANTS

¼ CUP OLIVE OIL

½ TEASPOON SUGAR

½ TEASPOON SALT

½ CUP WATER

8 OUNCES TOMATO CONCASSE*

GREASEPROOF COOKING PAPER

Stuffing

½ CUP OLIVE OIL

⅓ CUP PINE NUTS

6 MEDIUM ONIONS, FINELY GRATED

1 CUP RICE

1 TEASPOON SALT

BLACK PEPPER, FRESHLY GROUND, TO TASTE

1 TEASPOON CINNAMON

1 TEASPOON ALLSPICE

⅓ CUP BLACK CURRANTS, SOAKED IN SALTED WATER FOR 1 HOUR

1 TEASPOON SUGAR

1⅛ CUP HOT WATER

2 TABLESPOONS FLAT-LEAF PARSLEY, CHOPPED (RESERVE STALKS)

2 TABLESPOONS FRESH MINT, FINELY CHOPPED (RESERVE STALKS)

2 TABLESPOONS FRESH DILL, FINELY CHOPPED (RESERVE STALKS)

Prepare the stuffing first. Heat the olive oil in a pan. Add pine nuts and fry until lightly colored, stirring frequently. Add onions and continue stirring until tender. If necessary, add more olive oil. Add rice and cook another 3 minutes. Add salt, pepper, cinnamon, allspice, black currants, sugar and hot water. Mix well and bring to a boil. Cover and cook the stuffing very gently for 15 minutes. Remove from heat. Stir in herbs. Cover again and set aside for 15 minutes.

To prepare the eggplants for stuffing, cut off the stems. Separate the flesh from the skin by running a knife close to the skin at the cut stem end, penetrating as deeply

[Zetinyağlı Patlıcan Dolması, *continued*]

as possible without cutting the skin. To remove the loosened flesh, roll the eggplant vigorously between both hands, and then carefully ease the flesh out. Cut a ½ thick slice of the flesh from the stem end to use as a "plug."

Fill the eggplant "shells" with stuffing. Put the saved "plug" in the open end. Line the base of a deep pan with reserved parsley, mint and dill stalks. Place eggplants in the pan, side-by-side, stem end up. Mix together olive oil, sugar, salt and water, and pour over the eggplants. Add crushed tomato. Cover pan with greaseproof cooking paper and then with the lid. Simmer for 40–45 minutes. Remove pan from heat. Let cool, with the cover on. Remove eggplants and serve at room temperature.

*fresh tomatoes pounded or crushed into a coarse purée.

Zetinyağlı Yaprak Dolması

Stuffed vine leaves cooked in olive oil. Serves 12.

Tom Brosnahan, author of Lonely Planet's *Turkey: A Travel Survival Kit,* provided the recipe for this dish.

8 LARGE ONIONS, GRATED

½–1 CUP OLIVE OIL

4 TABLESPOONS PINE NUTS

1 CUP LONG GRAIN RICE, UNCOOKED

1 MEDIUM CAN CHOPPED TOMATOES

4 TABLESPOONS CURRANTS

2 CUPS HOT WATER

SALT AND PEPPER TO TASTE

1 BUNCH DILL, FINELY CHOPPED

½–⅔ POUND GRAPE LEAVES, PRESERVED (DRAINED WEIGHT)

1 LEMON

Grate the onions finely in a food processor. Heat olive oil in a large pot, then fry the onions and pine nuts for 10 minutes, stirring frequently. Add rice and cook for another five minutes. Add tomatoes with their juice, currants, one cup hot water, and salt and pepper. Stir once, cover and simmer over very low heat until liquid is absorbed (20–25 minutes). Stir in finely chopped dill and let cool.

Rinse and drain grape leaves. Line a large, deep frying pan with torn leaves. Place a whole leaf on the table with the stem toward you, matte side up. Trim the stem if more than ¼ inch long. Place a tablespoon of stuffing near the stem end and roll the leaf away from you to cover the stuffing. Then fold the sides of the leaf toward the center and finish rolling. Make a firm little roll.

Place the stuffed grape leaves in the frying pan, side-by-side; you may make two layers if necessary. Continue until you have used all the leaves. Pour one cup hot water and the juice of half a lemon over them. Cover with a plate, and put a lid on the frying pan. Simmer for 20–30 minutes. Pour off excess water and let cool. Transfer to a serving dish and garnish with lemon slices or wedges. Serve as an appetizer or as a separate (usually second) course with bread.

SOUPS

Arabaşi Çorbası

Arab's meal. Serves 5–6.

The recipe for this soup was contributed by Esra Levent, Director of IDEE Travel Services in İstanbul, who is from Mersin, a city on the eastern Mediterranean coast of Turkey.

> 1 MEDIUM-SIZED CHICKEN
>
> 1½ QUARTS WATER
>
> 2 TABLESPOONS FLOUR
>
> 1 TABLESPOON BUTTER
>
> 1 TABLESPOON TOMATO PASTE
>
> 1 TABLESPOON HOT PEPPER PASTE*
>
> PINCH OF SALT
>
> ½ TEASPOON BLACK PEPPER

Cut chicken into pieces and place in pan with 1½ quarts water. Bring to boil and then simmer 1 hour to make a rich broth. Shred the meat very finely. Save the broth. Brown the flour in butter. Add chicken broth to the flour, very slowly, stirring continuously. Thin tomato paste and hot pepper paste in a cup of the chicken broth and add it, with the shredded chicken, to the mixture. Bring the soup to boiling. Continue to boil for 10 minutes. Add salt and pepper, and serve piping hot.

*See *Resources* (p. 57) for mail-order suppliers. Can substitute a tablespoon of tomato paste and add ⅛ teaspoon cayenne pepper.

Yoğurt Çorbası

Eastern Anatolian yogurt soup. Serves 4–6.

Ayla Algar, author of *Classical Turkish Cooking,* provided the recipe for this soup.

> 6 CUPS GOOD CHICKEN OR MEAT STOCK
>
> ⅔ CUP HULLED WHEAT (OR BARLEY)

[Yoğurt Çorbası, *continued*]

> 3½ CUPS PLAIN YOGURT
>
> 3 TABLESPOONS FLOUR
>
> 2 EGG YOLKS
>
> 2 CUPS COLD WATER
>
> SALT
>
> 2–3 TABLESPOONS UNSALTED BUTTER
>
> ¼ CUP DRIED MINT LEAVES

Bring the stock to a boil in a large, heavy pan. Stir in the grain, cover, and simmer over medium heat for about 40 minutes, until the wheat is tender. In a large bowl, with a wooden spoon, mix the yogurt with the flour and egg yolks until smooth. Gradually mix in the cold water. Stir this into the soup through a sieve. Season with salt. Cover and simmer the soup gently for 10 minutes.

Heat the butter in a small saucepan until frothy. Sprinkle in the mint leaves, crushing with your fingertips as you add them. Stir and let the mixture sizzle a second or two; pour this into the soup. Serve hot. The mint can be added directly to the soup, omitting the butter, if desired. The soup keeps well and can be reheated for subsequent servings. It thickens as it stands; thin with water.

For variation, use ½ cup coarsely chopped fresh cilantro instead of mint, adding it directly to the soup just before removing it from the heat. It gives the soup an entirely different flavor.

SIDE DISHES

Sade Pilâv

Plain pilaf. Serves 8.
This recipe was provided by Selim S. Kuru, a graduate of Harvard, from İstanbul.

> 2 CUPS RICE (NOT THE JASMINE VARIETY)
>
> HOT WATER TO SOAK RICE
>
> 1 TEASPOON SALT
>
> 4 TABLESPOONS BUTTER
>
> 2 CUPS COLD WATER
>
> *Optional*[*]
>
> ½ CUP MUSHROOMS, CHOPPED
>
> ¼ CUP RAISINS

¼ CUP ALMONDS, SOAKED IN WATER OVERNIGHT†

¼ CUP BOILED CHESTNUTS, CUT IN HALF AND SOAKED IN WATER
OVERNIGHT†

1 SMALL ONION, CHOPPED

2 TOMATOES, CHOPPED

Put rice in bowl and cover for 20 minutes with hot water and salt. Then wash the rice with cold water until the water is clear, and drain. Fry butter in a saucepan until it just begins to brown. Add rice and fry, stirring continuously. When the rice begins to stick to the pan, add 2 cups cold water and bring to boil on high heat. Do not stir. Then reduce the heat to medium and continue cooking until water level is at the surface of the rice. Then simmer until rice begins to stick to the pan.

Put a paper towel inside a tightly fitting pan lid to prevent condensed water forming on it from dropping on the rice to make it soggy, and cover the rice. Then remove the pan from the heat and let sit, covered, for 10–15 minutes. Stir before serving, using a wooden spoon so the rice grains won't get broken.

*If optional ingredients are desired, they should be added to the rice prior to frying it. Use any desired combination; amounts are suggestions. If tomatoes are added, they go best with just onions.

†Soaking tenderizes them and facilitates removal of the skin.

SALADS

Patlıcan Salatası

Eggplant salad. Serves 10.

The recipe for this salad was contributed by İstanbul native Ayşe Somersan, former Professor of Agricultural Economics at the University of Wisconsin and former Dean and Director of Wisconsin's Cooperative Extension System.

2 LONG, THIN MEDIUM-SIZED EGGPLANTS

2 GREEN PEPPERS, CUT IN 1-INCH STRIPS

2 TOMATOES, QUARTERED AND SEEDED

3–4 CLOVES GARLIC, DICED

OLIVE OR OTHER VEGETABLE OIL FOR FRYING

½ CUP BALSAMIC OR WINE VINEGAR, OR A MIXTURE OF BOTH

Peel eggplants lengthwise, alternating ½-inch strips of peeled and unpeeled sections to create a striped eggplant. Slice into ¼-inch (or thinner) round sections. Put in salt water for 2 hours to remove bitterness. Drain well on paper towels. Fry in hot oil until dark brown on both sides. Drain well on paper towels. Fry green pepper strips

[Patlıcan Salatası, *continued*]

until soft and light brown. Cut off their curved ends for more even frying. Remove from pan and drain well on paper towels. Then fry the tomatoes for a few minutes. Watch out for sputtering oil. Arrange vegetables in a deep serving bowl. Sprinkle with garlic. Drizzle vinegar over everything and refrigerate until cold.

MAIN DISHES

Etli Yeşil Fasulye

Green beans with lamb. Serves 3–4.

The recipe for this typical Turkish dish was provided by Wynne Oz. The dish was adapted to American ingredients.

3 TABLESPOONS OLIVE OIL

4 LARGE LAMB SHOULDER CHOPS (OR 2 POUNDS OF LEG OF LAMB), CUT IN
   SMALL PIECES

1 PAT OF BUTTER

3 CLOVES GARLIC

2 MEDIUM ONIONS, CHOPPED

2 BEEF BOUILLON CUBES

½ TEASPOON PAPRIKA

½ TEASPOON OREGANO

½ TEASPOON THYME

¼ TEASPOON ROSEMARY

¼ TEASPOON BASIL

¼ TEASPOON MARJORAM

¼ TEASPOON SAGE

SALT AND PEPPER TO TASTE

2 LARGE, RIPE TOMATOES, ONE CHOPPED, ONE SLICED

1 8-OUNCE CAN V8 JUICE

1 CUP WATER

2 POUNDS FRESH GREEN BEANS

In a large, heavy casserole, heat the olive oil. Sauté meat on high heat until brown, about 5 minutes. Remove meat from pot and set aside. Pour out and discard the oil and fat. To the same pot, add pat of butter and sauté garlic and onions. Turn heat to low and return meat to pot. Add bouillon cubes and season to taste. Add chopped tomato, V8 juice and ½ cup water. Cover tightly and cook on very low heat for about an hour. Meat should be very tender. Add another ½ cup water and green beans, with ends snipped. Place tomato slices on top of beans. Cover and cook on low heat until beans are tender. To enhance flavor, cook in advance and refrigerate a few hours. Reheat to serve.

Adana Kebabı

Spicy kebab, a specialty of the province of Adana in the eastern Mediterranean region of Turkey. Serves 2.

The recipe for this dish was provided by Bora Özkök, from Adana, who heads Cultural Folk Tours International, a company in California specializing in tours to Turkey. You will need flat skewers with blades from ¾ inch to 1½ inches wide. See *Resources* (p. 57) for mail-order suppliers.

> 1 POUND GROUND LAMB
>
> 1 LARGE ONION, FINELY CHOPPED
>
> 1 CUP LOOSELY PACKED FLAT-LEAF PARSLEY, FINELY CHOPPED
>
> 1 CLOVE GARLIC, MINCED
>
> ½ TEASPOON CRUSHED RED PEPPER FLAKES*
>
> ¼ TEASPOON SALT
>
> ⅛ TEASPOON BLACK PEPPER, FRESHLY GROUND
>
> 2 TOMATOES, QUARTERED
>
> 6 LONG, THIN GREEN PEPPERS
>
> TURKISH FLAT BREAD, OR *PIDE*†
>
> MELTED BUTTER
>
> *Relish*
>
> 1 RED ONION, CUT IN PAPER-THIN SLICES
>
> FLAT-LEAF PARSLEY (USE A FEW UNCUT SPRIGS FROM ABOVE)
>
> ½ TABLESPOON *SUMAK*††

Mix well the meat, onion, parsley, garlic, red pepper flakes, salt and pepper. Divide mixture into 4 balls; each will be about the size of a large egg. Place one of the pieces at the lower end of a skewer, which should be held upright. Squeeze the meat so it completely surrounds the blade. The object is to mold this ball into a long sausage shape around the blade. Begin by grasping the lower end of the ball with your hand, coaxing the portion within the hand to conform to the contours of the blade. Then move your hand a short distance up and squeeze the next portion

[Adana Kebabı, *continued*]

of meat. Continue until all the meat has been closely squeezed around the skewer, and is now sausage shaped.

Grill until well done. Then grill the tomatoes and peppers. Warm the flat bread and break it into pieces. Put some on each plate and drizzle it with melted butter. On each plate lay two kebabs on top of the bread. Put tomatoes and peppers on top of the kebabs. To make the relish, mix the onion slices with parsley and *sumak* and serve on the same platter with the kebabs.

*See *Resources* (p. 57) for mail-order suppliers. Can substitute ½ teaspoon cayenne pepper.

†See *Resources* (p. 57) for mail-order suppliers.

††See *Foods & Flavors Guide* (p. 103). For mail-order suppliers, see *Resources* (p. 57).

Etli Biber Dolması

Stuffed green peppers. Serves 5.

The recipe for this dish was provided by Hüsnü Atış, who comes from Erzurum, a city in northeastern Anatolia. He is the owner and chef of Hüsnü's, a Turkish restaurant in Madison, Wisconsin.

> 5 LARGE GREEN BELL PEPPERS
>
> 1 POUND GROUND LAMB (OR BEEF)
>
> 1 CUP UNCOOKED RICE
>
> 1 ONION, CHOPPED
>
> 1 6-OUNCE CAN TOMATO PASTE
>
> ½ CUP FLAT-LEAF PARSLEY, CHOPPED
>
> 1 TEASPOON CUMIN
>
> PINCH CAYENNE PEPPER
>
> 1 CLOVE GARLIC, CRUSHED
>
> 1 TEASPOON SALT
>
> 1 TEASPOON PEPPER
>
> 2 TEASPOONS OREGANO
>
> LETTUCE LEAVES
>
> YOGURT

Cut tops off green peppers and save. Wash peppers, remove seeds and set aside. Combine meat, rice, onion, tomato paste, parsley, cumin, cayenne, garlic, salt and pepper in a large mixing bowl. Mix well and stuff the mixture into the peppers.

To cook, use a pot that will allow the peppers to fit in snugly so they don't fall over. Line the pot with lettuce leaves to prevent the peppers from sticking to the bottom. Fill the pot with water to submerge the bottom half of the peppers. Put the tops on the filled peppers. Add tomato paste and oregano to cooking liquid. Bake at 350°F for 60 minutes or until the rice is tender. To serve, top the peppers with yogurt.

Kabak Böreği

Zucchini börek. Serves 10.

This recipe was contributed by Christine Ogan, professor of journalism at Indiana University, in memory of her mother-in-law, Hasbiye Ogan, from İstanbul, who often made this dish. The family fondly calls this preparation *maşallah böreği.* They utter the exclamation *"maşallah"* when the *börek* is removed from the oven because it puffs up so high in the center. In Arabic, this expression means "what God wills," and in Turkey, it is used as an expression of admiration, amazement or good will.

Filling

3–4 LARGE ZUCCHINI, SHREDDED

SALT

4 EGGS

1 BUNCH DILL, FINELY CHOPPED

1 BUNCH FLAT-LEAF PARSLEY, FINELY CHOPPED

BLACK PEPPER, FRESHLY GROUND TO TASTE

Dough*

4 CUPS UNBLEACHED WHITE FLOUR

1 TEASPOON SALT

1⅓ CUP LUKEWARM WATER

¼ CUP OLIVE OR OTHER VEGETABLE OIL

Coating for dough

1 CUP YOGURT

½–¾ CUP MELTED BUTTER

2 BEATEN EGGS

Sprinkle the zucchini with salt and place in a colander to drain for about two hours. Then squeeze out all the liquid possible and combine with the eggs, herbs and black pepper.

To make the dough, place all ingredients in a food processor and blend until well-kneaded, like bread dough. It should take about 2 minutes. Add more flour or

[Kabak Böreği, *continued*]

water if needed. Place in an oiled bowl, covered, for about 1 hour at room temperature. Divide pastry into 10–12 pieces, depending on the size of the pan you will use for the *börek*. The pan size should be at least 9 by 13 inches. The smaller the pan, the thicker the *börek*. Keep pieces of dough covered with a towel until used. To roll out, use a 1-inch piece of doweling. The Turks use a long, round stick called an *oklava* (see *Foods & Flavors Guide,* p. 103). Dust a counter top with flour and roll out each piece to about 14 by 18 inches, dusting with flour as needed. This will not be easy for beginners. Roll the dough as big as possible, then pick it up and try to stretch out the parts that couldn't be rolled well. Place it back on the counter and continue rolling. Don't worry if holes form in the pastry. They can be patched and won't matter anyway when the dough is put into the pan. Place each finished piece on a cloth, and cover with a light dusting of flour and a piece of wax paper. Continue to stack them until all are rolled out, separating each with a piece of wax paper. When all are rolled, lightly oil a pan for baking.

To make the coating for the dough, combine yogurt, butter and eggs in a bowl and set aside.

To assemble *börek,* place a piece of rolled dough (or half a sheet of prepared pastry*) in the bottom of the greased pan. The dough can be wrinkled up so that it fits in evenly. Brush with the yogurt, butter and egg mixture. Place another piece of dough (or prepared pastry) on top. Repeat until half the pieces of dough have been used. Put the filling on top and spread evenly over the dough. Then continue the layering process with the rest of the dough. Make sure to reserve enough of the yogurt, butter and egg mixture to generously coat the top layer.

Bake at 350°F until puffed and golden; about 1 hour if using a 9 by 13 inch pan and hand-rolled dough. Say "*maşallah*" as you remove it from the oven. As the *börek* rests the top will flatten.

*Ready-made pastry sheets, called *yufka,* are available in several stores supplying foods from the Middle East. See *Resources* (p. 57) for mail-order suppliers.

Ali Nazik Kebabı

Eggplant puree with yogurt and ground meat. Serves 4.

This recipe was provided by Mustafa Siyahhan, former director of the Turkish Information Office in Washington, D.C., who is from Şanlıurfa, a city in southeastern Anatolia. This recipe is a variation of the famous recipe *hünkâr beğendi* (see *Menu Guide,* p. 82).

> 4 LONG, THIN MEDIUM-SIZED EGGPLANTS
>
> 1 TABLESPOON OIL
>
> 2½ CUPS YOGURT
>
> 3 CLOVES GARLIC, MINCED

1 TEASPOON SALT

1 POUND GROUND LAMB (OR BEEF)

1 TABLESPOON BUTTER

½ TEASPOON SALT

½ TEASPOON PEPPER

½ TEASPOON RED PEPPER

1 LARGE GREEN BELL PEPPER, CHOPPED

Roast the eggplants over a flame to char the skin. Cool. Peel skin and mince the flesh. Sauté in oil for 3 minutes, stirring continuously. Add yogurt, garlic and salt and mix thoroughly. Set aside, keeping warm. Brown the meat in butter. Drain. Add salt and spices. Evenly spread the eggplant mixture in a shallow serving dish. Arrange the ground meat mixture in the center. Top with green pepper and serve warm.

Sultan Sarma

Tenderloin wrapped around a filling of mushrooms, pistachios and cheese. Serves 2. The recipe for this dish was contributed by Ömer Çeliksoy, former service manager of the Hotel Cappadocia Dedeman in Nevşehir, a city in central Anatolia. Mr. Çeliksoy is from Mengen, a city in northcentral Anatolia. Turkey's most renowned chef's school, where he received his training, is located there.

1 POUND TENDERLOIN, SLICED CROSSWISE INTO 6 PIECES, POUNDED THIN

3 LARGE MUSHROOMS, CHOPPED

1 SMALL ONION, FINELY CHOPPED

3 TABLESPOONS OIL

1 TABLESPOON PISTACHIOS, WHOLE

½ CUP *KAŞAR* CHEESE, GRATED*

SALT AND PEPPER TO TASTE

¼ TEASPOON PAPRIKA

Pound the tenderloin into thin pieces. Fry the mushrooms and onion in oil until brown. Remove from heat and add pistachios, cheese and spices. Put a heaping tablespoon of stuffing on each piece of meat. Roll the meat around the stuffing. Secure with toothpicks, if necessary. Grill. Do not overcook.

*See *Resources* (p. 57) for mail-order suppliers. Can substitute with a pale, mild or medium cheddar.

Malatya Usülü Fasulye Yaprağı Dolması

Stuffed green bean leaves, cooked in the style of Malatya. Serves 3–4.

Elizabet Narin Kurumlu provided this recipe, which she obtained for us from her grandmother, Eliz Kurumlu. Both are from Malatya, a city in eastern Anatolia known for the ingenious use of many different varieties of leaves to wrap around meat or meatless stuffings. Malatya is also the apricot capital of Turkey.

20 GREEN BEAN LEAVES, OF UNIFORM SIZE

¾ CUP CRACKED WHEAT

⅓ CUP BULGUR, FINELY GROUND

½ TEASPOON SALT

½ CUP WATER

Sauce

8 OUNCES PLAIN YOGURT

1 TABLESPOON FLOUR

2 TABLESPOONS SOUR PLUM PASTE* OR LEMON JUICE

½ CUP WATER

Roux

2 TABLESPOONS FLOUR

1 TABLE SPOON BUTTER

¾ TEASPOONS SALT

Topping

1 LARGE ONIONS, CHOPPED

1–2 TABLESPOONS MELTED BUTTER

Wash the bean leaves and make a notch about ¼ inch from the stem edge to remove both the tough, thick part of the center rib and the stem. Mix together the cracked wheat, bulgur and salt. Slowly add water. Using the hands, knead the mixture for about 20 minutes to form a stiff paste. When ready, place about ⅔ tablespoon of the paste near the stem edge of the leaf. Have the matte side of the leaf up and the stem edge facing you. Roll the leaf away from you to cover the stuffing. Then fold in the sides to the center and finish rolling. Make a tight roll so it does not unfold during cooking and float to the surface. Stuff 15 leaves.

To cook, use a saucepan small enough to have the rolls fit snugly together. Line pan with 5 leaves to prevent sticking. Arrange the rolls on top. Add enough cool water just to cover them. Place an earthenware plate upside down on top of them. Bring water to boil over medium heat and boil for 1–2 minutes. Pour water off without disturbing the rolls. Repeat this process 3 more times, always starting with cool water. Prepare the sauce by mixing the yogurt and flour with plum paste or lemon juice.

Add water and mix thoroughly. Pour this mixture over the drained rolls. Add more water to raise the level of the yogurt mixture 1 inch over the top of the rolls. Bring to boil on medium heat. In a separate bowl, make a roux with flour, butter and salt. To this mixture, add a few tablespoons of the yogurt sauce in the saucepan, making a smooth paste. Add to yogurt mixture when it begins to boil, gently stirring it in. Continue to cook over medium heat for about 10–12 minutes.

While the stuffed leaves are cooking, fry the onion in butter until lighly browned and set aside. When the rolls are cooked, place in a serving dish with the yogurt sauce and top with the fried onion mixture.

This dish typically is served with fresh red onions on the side. It is followed with a *hoşaf*, or cold compote, usually made from dried or fresh plums, a preparation traditionally thought to aid digestion of the bean leaves.

*See *Resources* (p. 57) for mail-order suppliers.

Kabak Kalye

Zucchini with ground meat. Serves 4–5.

The recipe for this dish was contributed by Nurdan Uyan, from İstanbul, who lives with her family in Wisconsin.

> 2 POUNDS ZUCCHINI
>
> 3 CUPS BOILING WATER
>
> SALT
>
> ½ POUND GROUND BEEF OR LAMB
>
> 2 ONIONS, GRATED
>
> 2 TABLESPOONS BUTTER
>
> 2 TOMATOES, SLICED
>
> 1 GREEN PEPPER, SEEDED AND CHOPPED
>
> ¼ CUP DILL, CHOPPED
>
> ¼ CUP FRESH MINT, CHOPPED
>
> SALT AND PEPPER TO TASTE
>
> DASH CAYENNE
>
> ½ CUP BROTH

Peel and cut each zucchini crosswise into 4 or more pieces. Cook in 3 cups boiling, salted water for 3 minutes. Drain and place in one layer in a shallow cooking pan. Sauté meat and onions in butter over medium heat for 5 minutes, stirring constantly. Add tomatoes and green peppers and sauté for another 5 minutes. Remove from

[Kabak kalye, *continued*]
heat and spread over the zucchini. Place dill and mint on top, add salt, black pepper and cayenne. Add broth. Cover and cook over medium heat for 30–35 minutes. Serve hot with egg noodles.

DESSERTS

Sütlâç

Rice pudding. Serves 12.
This recipe was provided by Ali Kemal Dinçer, a business owner in Belmont, MA, who is from Gaziantep, a city in southeastern Turkey.

>   1 CUP LONG-GRAIN RICE
>
>   1 CUP GRANULATED SUGAR
>
>   10 CUPS WHOLE MILK
>
>   1 TEASPOON VANILLA EXTRACT
>
>   CINNAMON

Mix the first four ingredients in a large saucepan. Bring to boil on medium to hot heat, stirring occasionally. Immediately reduce heat. Continue boiling for 1½–2 hours, or until a pudding consistency is reached. If not boiled long enough, the rice grains remain too hard. Put in individual cups or shallow serving dish, cover top and chill before serving. To serve, sprinkle with cinnamon. If desired, orange zest, cinnamon, cloves or rose water can be used instead of, or in addition to, vanilla.

Aşure

Noah's pudding. Serves 8–10.
This recipe was contributed by Leyla Özhan, former Director of the New York Turkish Tourism Office, who is from Çorum, a city in central Anatolia.

>   ¾ CUP HULLED WHOLE WHEAT (WHEAT BERRIES)
>
>   ⅓ CUP WHITE BEANS, DRIED
>
>   ⅓ CUP CHICKPEAS
>
>   ¼ CUP RICE
>
>   1½ CUPS SUGAR
>
>   10 FIGS, DRIED
>
>   10 APRICOTS, DRIED
>
>   ⅓ CUP RAISINS

2 TABLESPOONS ROSE WATER

⅓ CUP WALNUT PIECES

⅓ CUP PISTACHIOS

SEEDS FROM ONE SMALL POMEGRANATE

Soak the wheat, beans and chickpeas in water overnight in separate bowls. Next day, rinse, drain and boil each separately in fresh water until tender, stirring occasionally. Remove from heat and drain, saving the combined cooking liquids. Put wheat, beans and chickpeas in 2½ quarts of the saved liquid, adding water if necessary. Add rice and simmer 60 minutes. Add sugar and simmer until dissolved. Soak figs and apricots in some hot water for a few minutes. Drain and cut into small pieces. Add to simmering mixture, along with raisins. Simmer for another 10 minutes. Remove from heat and stir in rose water. Serve chilled in individual dessert bowls garnished with walnuts, pistachios and pomegranate seeds.

Künefe

A syrup-soaked, cheese-filled dessert pastry. Serves 8.

The recipe for this delicious dessert was provided by İstanbul native Irvin C. Schick, who lives in Massachusetts.

2 CUPS SUGAR

1¼ CUPS WATER

1 TABLESPOON LEMON JUICE

1 POUND PASTRY STRANDS, OR *TEL KADAYIF**

8 OUNCES UNSALTED BUTTER, MELTED (USE MORE IF NEEDED)

1–1½ POUNDS UNSALTED CHEESE, GRATED (CAN USE MOZARELLA)

Preheat oven to 350°F. Combine sugar and water in a saucepan. Dissolve the sugar over low heat, stirring continuously. Allow mixture to gently boil for 5 minutes. Add lemon juice and boil another minute. Set aside to cool to room temperature. Take small clumps of the thread-like pastry dough and thoroughly soak them in melted butter. If it is not soaked well, it will burn.

Divide the butter-soaked pastry in half. Lay one half at the bottom and sides of a buttered 8 or 10 inch pan (round or square). Cover with cheese. Top with the remaining buttered pastry. Bake at 350°F for 45 minutes, then at 450°F for another 15 minutes.

Remove it from the oven if it begins to turn brown. It must be a deep gold color. Invert the pan and release the dessert onto a serving dish. Immediately drown with the cooled syrup and serve hot.

*See *Resources* (p. 57) for mail-order suppliers.

İrmik Helvası

Semolina halvah. Serves 8–10.

This adaptation of a popular dessert was provided by Ali Kemal Dinçer, a business owner in Belmont, MA, who is from Gaziantep, a city in southeastern Turkey.

2 CUPS WHOLE MILK

1¼ CUPS GRANULATED SUGAR

½ CUP UNSALTED BUTTER

¼ VEGETABLE OIL

¼ CUP PINE NUTS

1 CUP SEMOLINA (LARGEST-SIZED GRAIN AVAILABLE)

Bring milk, sugar and butter to boil in a medium-size saucepan. Set aside or keep on low heat. Put vegetable oil and pine nuts in a large saucepan and cook over moderate heat until bubbles form. Cook nuts until lightly browned, about 1 minute. Add semolina and stir vigorously for 3–6 minutes. If a darker halvah is preferred, cook a few minutes longer. It will begin to burn at about 10 minutes.

Slowly add the milk, sugar and butter to the nuts and semolina. The mixture will start to boil rapidly, so watch out for spattering. Stir continuously over moderate heat for several minutes until thickened but still fluid. Pour into a shallow, 9-inch pie dish, and cool until set, about 2 hours. To serve, cut into pieces. For variation, slivered almonds or unsalted pistachios can be substituted for pine nuts.

İrmiki Hurma Tatlısı

Date-shaped semolina dessert cookies. Makes about 3 dozen.

This recipe was provided by Nurten Tabur, wife of Feridun Tabur, former assistant general manager at the Hotel Dedeman in Antalya on the Mediterranean coast. It is a special dessert from her hometown, İzmit, in the Sea of Marmara region of Turkey.

Sugar syrup

2⅔ CUP SUGAR

2⅓ CUPS WATER

1 TABLESPOON LEMON JUICE, FRESHLY SQUEEZED

Dough

⅔ CUP MARGARINE

⅔ CUP MILK

⅔ CUP SUGAR

½ TEASPOON BAKING SODA

½ TEASPOON VANILLA EXTRACT

⅓ CUP SEMOLINA

2⅔ CUPS UNBLEACHED FLOUR

⅔ CUPS WALNUTS, VERY FINELY CHOPPED

GRATED COCONUT OR FINELY CHOPPED PISTACHIOS FOR DECORATION

Preheat oven to 325°F. Prepare syrup first. Boil sugar and water 10 minutes. Remove from burner and add lemon juice. Bring to boil again and let cool. To prepare dough, melt margarine in saucepan and remove from heat. Add milk, sugar, baking soda and vanilla. Mix well. Stir in semolina. Slowly add flour and mix well. To make cookies, form an oval from 1 tablespoon dough. Make a lengthwise groove and fill it with ground walnuts. Pinch dough together around the nuts. Bake on lightly oiled cookie sheet about 30 minutes, or until light brown. Remove cookies from oven and pour cool syrup over them. When the syrup is absorbed, remove cookies from pan and decorate with coconut or pistachios.

MISCELLANEOUS

Ezme Salatası

Spicy tomato salad, a relish served with grilled or barbecued meat. Serves 8.

This recipe was provided by Ressan Süzek, former director of the New York Turkish Tourist Office. She is from Ankara, the capital of Turkey, in central Anatolia.

2 MEDIUM, RIPE TOMATOES, PEELED

2-INCH PIECE OF CUCUMBER, PEELED

1 GREEN BELL PEPPER

2 SCALLIONS

¼ TEASPOON DRIED MINT

½ TEASPOON PAPRIKA

½ TEASPOON BLACK PEPPER, FRESHLY GROUND

½ TEASPOON SALT

1 TABLESPOON RED WINE VINEGAR

1 TABLESPOON OLIVE OIL

Remove the seeds of the tomatoes, cucumber and pepper. Chop vegetables into very fine pieces, using a sharp knife or a mini-food processor. Drain excess liquid. Add remaining ingredients and mix well. Make a few hours ahead for fuller flavor.

Yoğurt

Yogurt.

This food, a product of milk curdled by a specific culture of bacteria, is a ubiquitous ingredient of Turkish cuisine. Fermenting milk as a means of preserving it has been used since ancient times.

YOGURT, WITHOUT FAT REMOVED

WHOLE MILK

To prepare, obtain a starter culture from a friend or buy a good brand of yogurt without the fat removed, which contains the live culture of bacteria. Use yogurt and whole milk in the proportion of 1 part yogurt to 10 parts milk. To prepare, gently bring milk to a boil. Cool to the point where your finger can be kept in the mixture for 10 seconds. Then transfer to a bowl. Dilute yogurt with a small amount of the heated milk and then add it to the milk in the bowl. Cover tightly. Wrap in a heavy towel or woolen blanket. After about 12 hours, the mixture should be thick. Refrigerate and do not disturb until chilled. Then pour off any liquid on the top. If you wait too long to refrigerate the yogurt, it will become somewhat sour.

To make a thicker yogurt resembling soft cheese, drain chilled yogurt in a strainer or through a piece of cheesecloth for a few hours in the refrigerator.

BEVERAGES

Türk Kahvesi

Turkish coffee. Serves 2.

To brew Turkish coffee you will need a *cezve,* a long-handled, wide-necked pot available in many sizes. For mail-order suppliers, see *Resources* (p. 57). You will need demitasses for serving.

TURKISH COFFEE, FINELY PULVERIZED

SUGAR

COLD WATER

Put 2 demitasse-size cupfuls of water (about 4 ounces) in a 2-cup *cezve.* Note that it is important to use the correct size *cezve* to ensure that enough froth will form for the required number of cups. Add 1 teaspoon each of coffee and sugar* per cup to the *cezve.* Mix well. Put on low heat and slowly bring to a boil. Do not stir. As it begins to boil, a thick froth forms on the top. Just before it overflows, remove the pot from the heat and carefully pour an equal amount of froth into each cup. Return pot to stove and bring just to boiling point again. Pour coffee into cups without disturbing the froth in them. Let the sediment settle before sipping.

*or to taste.

Shopping in Turkey's Food Markets

Helpful Tips

The Open-Air Markets

Learning more about Turkish food in an outdoor market setting is fascinating. These markets, or *pazar*, typically are centrally located. They are held on a specific day of the week and are set up and dismantled the same day. Be sure to look for regional food item specialities. Typically, non-food items also will be available. Hand-carved cooking spoons made out of a hard wood called *şimşir* are especially nice.

To get a feeling for how purchases are negotiated, stroll around the rows of food stalls and watch the lively interaction between the vendors and the local people. There can be some haggling over prices, but you will discover that the prices already are quite reasonable. Your time would be better spent saving dollars elsewhere rather than a penny or two here. If prices are not marked, however, it would be wise to see what the local folk pay so you don't end up paying a lot more.

Food in the markets is sold by weight (grams). To encourage sales, vendors often offer generous samples to taste. This is a good opportunity to ask for the name of an item that is not labelled. If you would like to give the Turkish language a try, see *Helpful Phrases* (p. 65). The vendors, and many of the other Turks around you, will be happy to answer questions.

Some of the more unusual items in the outdoor markets are exotic spices and the many herbs used as restoratives. Examples of spices generally unfamiliar to Americans are *mahleb, sahleb, sumak* and *sakız*. See *Foods & Flavors Guide* (p. 103). Curative teas are made from a variety of dried plants such as *ıhlamur* (linden blossoms), which is used as a cold remedy.

The Supermarkets

Be sure to shop in the large supermarkets, or *gıda pazarı*. They are a great place to get the makings for a tasty picnic featuring Turkish food. There are many tempting varieties of sausages and cheeses, some of them regional specialties, at the meat counter. Try *pastırma,* the salted and dried meat cured with a spicy paste called *çemen,* and *çökelek,* a soft cheese made from skim milk. And for convenience, before leaving home, pack some tableware and a pocket knife!

Meat and cheese are sold by weight, measured in grams (1000 grams equals one kilogram). The following abbreviated list of weights in Turkish has proven sufficient to get the quantities we desired. Corresponding approximate weights in pounds are included.

125 grams: *yüz yirmi beş gram*	~	⅓ pound
250 grams: *iki yüz elli gram*	~	½ pound
500 grams (half kilo): *yarım kilo*	~	1 pound
750 grams: *yedi yüz elli gram*	~	1½ pound

If you are considering bringing food back to the United States, obtain the USDA-APHIS brochure "Travelers' Tips" beforehand to see which items are allowed. It is available online at www.aphis.usda.gov/travel/usdatips.html or by writing to:

USDA-APHIS "Travelers' Tips" Brochure #1083
Plant Protection & Quarantine / Marketing & Regulatory Programs
4700 River Road, Unit 133
Riverdale, MD 20737

A Health Precaution

Don't ask for trouble. Some serious diseases can be transmitted by eating unclean produce. If you buy fruits and vegetables in the markets, make sure to wash them thoroughly before eating. The safest fruits are those that can be peeled. Avoid eating food from street vendors. Bottled water is readily available and is a wise choice, even in restaurants.

Resources

Mail-Order Suppliers of Turkish Food Items

Some Turkish ingredients can be found in Middle Eastern food stores in metropolitan areas and in university towns with large foreign student populations. One generally can find meat products (*sucuk* and *pastırma*), spices (*sakız* and *sumak*), various doughs (*yufka* and *kadayıf*), cheeses (*beyaz peynir*) and Turkish coffee. Cookbooks and cooking utensils such as coffee grinders and the pot used to brew coffee, the *cezve,* are usually available, too.

Several mail-order suppliers of Turkish foods are listed below. Most of these stores do not have a catalog, but many carry most of the ingredients used in the recipes and will ship them to you. Please let us know if you discover that any of these stores has gone out of business since this book was printed.

Turkish food items also can be purchased online from several websites. An example is http://bestturkishfood.com. A list of Turkish grocery stores is found at http:///turkishconnection.com/food.htm. Since websites change or often are not updated with regularity, you will probably need to do additional browsing. We suggest that you use your favorite search engine (our standby is google.com) and do a general search for Turkish food markets or a specific search for a certain ingredient.

Sultan's Delight
PO Box 090302
Brooklyn, NY 11209
Tel: 800-852-5046 (orders only)
Tel: 718-745-2121
Fax: 718-745-2563
Check or charge
www.sultansdelight.com

Sunny Grocery
45-26 43rd Ave.
Sunnyside, NY 11104
Tel: 800-734-5636
Tel: 718-937-6256
Fax: 718-392-2528
No minimum order
Charge

Ari's Deli & Market
10515 McFadden #101-104
Garden Grove, CA 92643
Tel: 714-531-2747
Fax: 714-531-0253
C.O.D.

Sahara Mart
106 E 2nd St.
Bloomington, IN 47401
Tel: 812-333-0502
Minimum order $30
Charge

To buy *rakı,* the national liquor of Turkey, and a nice variety of fine Turkish wines, contact:

Potomac Wines and Spirits
3100 M St., NW
Washington, DC 20007
Tel: 202-333-2848
Fax: 202-625-1180
Request price list by fax.

Some Useful Organizations to Know About

We are members of two international organizations that exist to promote good will and understanding between people of different cultures. Since both groups have enriched our travel experiences considerably, we would like our readers to know about them. These organizations, Servas and The Friendship Force, share similar ideals but operate somewhat differently.

The other organizations we mention, tourist bureaus and travel agencies, cater specifically to Turkey-bound tourists. Some agencies listed have established tours with itineraries focusing on cuisine; others are currently planning them. All will assist travelers preferring independent travel to plan a custom itinerary highlighting Turkish cuisine. Information is also provided about the culinary tours led by Joan Peterson, author of this book.

Note that culinary tours typically also include many other activities, such as visits to major historical and archeological sights of Turkey. Inquire for details. Changes to itineraries can occur.

Servas

Servas, from the Esperanto word meaning "serve," is a non-profit system of travelers and hosts. Servas members travel independently and make their own contacts with fellow members in other countries, choosing hosts with attributes of interest from membership rosters. It is a wonderful way to get to know people, be invited into their homes as a family member, share experiences and help promote world peace. Visits usually are for two days. Some members are available only as "day hosts," but these shorter visits, too, are rewarding. The same welcome is extended to Servas members visiting the United States. Members of Servas in the United States generally are not organized into clubs at the local or state level.

U.S. Servas Committee, Inc.
11 John St., Room 505
New York, NY 10038
Tel: 212-267-0252
Fax: 212-267-0292
www.usservas.org
info@usservas.org

The Friendship Force

The Friendship Force is a non-profit organization, which also fosters good will through encounters between people of different backgrounds. Unlike Servas, Friendship Force members travel in groups to host countries. Both itinerary and travel arrangements are made by a member acting as exchange director. These trips combine stays with a host family and group travel within the host country. Friendship Force members are organized on the local level, and each club is involved in several incoming and outgoing exchanges during the year.

The Friendship Force
34 Peachtree St., Suite 900
Atlanta, GA 30303
Tel: 404-522-9490
Fax: 404-688-6148
www.friendshipforce.org
info@friendshipforce.org

Turkish Tourism Offices

Two offices of tourism can assist you with your travel planning. Maps and many up-to-date brochures packed with information about any area in the country you wish to visit are available. You will be amazed at the variety; the Turks are really serious about making you feel welcome. To request travel materials, write or call either office:

Turkish Tourism Office
2525 Massachusetts Ave., NW
Washington, DC 20008
Tel: 877-FOR TURKEY
Tel: 202-612-6800/6802
Fax: 202-319-7446
www.tourismturkey.org
dc@tourismturkey.org

Turkish Tourism Office
821 United Nations Plaza
New York, NY 10017
Tel: 877-FOR TURKEY
Tel: 212-687-2194
Fax: 212-599-7568
www.tourismturkey.org
ny@tourismturkey.org

EAT SMART Culinary Tours

Joan Peterson, world-wide traveler and author of the EAT SMART series of travel guides, leads the culinary tour "Eat Smart in Turkey." The tour is an exotic gourmet odyssey through Byzantine, Ottoman and modern Turkey. Tour participants also meet with renowned culinary experts, watch cooking demonstrations and have the opportunity to dine in Turkish homes for a rich introduction to Turkish regional cuisine. The itinerary includes Istanbul, the Aegean, the Mediterranean and Central Anatolia.

Contact Joan Peterson at ginkgo@ginkgopress.com and also visit www.ginkgopress.com for tour information as well as a photo gallery of images of previous tours.

IDEE Travel Services

This destination management company features a culinary tour called "Flavors of Anatolia." Centered in İstanbul, it includes dining experiences in world-famous restaurants showcasing the infinite varieties of classic and regional Turkish cuisine. Another culinary excursion is available to Cappadocia in central Anatolia. A variety of cooking classes also are offered.

For more information, write or call:

Turkish Office
IDEE Travel Services
Büyükdere Caddesi
Kaya Aldoğan Sokak No. 12/1
80300 Zincirlikuyu-İstanbul, Turkey
Tel: 011-90-212-275-8226
Fax: 011-90-212-275-1867
www.ideetravel.com

US Office
IDEE Travel Services
507 W. Barry Ave.
Chicago, IL 60657
Tel: 773-528-7002
info@ideetravel.com

Cultural Folk Tours International

The food tour of this agency, "The Turkish Gastronomical Delight Tour," is available as a private tour upon request. It begins in İstanbul and covers several north-central and central Anatolian cities, providing experiences ranging from gourmet to village cookery. Travelers will visit the famous chef's school in Mengen, and gain additional expertise by visiting Turkish kitchens and taking cooking lessons from Turkish chefs. These tours are led by company president Bora Özkök, considered somewhat of a pied piper because he plays his many musical instruments throughout the tour.

For more information, write or call:

Cultural Folk Tours International
5631 Lincoln Ave., #B
Cypress, CA 90630
Tel: 800-935-TURK
Tel: 714-252-9072
Fax: 714-252-9137
www.boraozkok.com
tourinfo@boraozkok.com

Newport International Travel

"Turkish Delights: A Culinary Tour of Turkey" is the name of this agency's food tour, which takes off from İstanbul and covers many cities in central Anatolia and the Aegean region. Travelers experience the rich and varied cuisine in renowned restaurants and in Turkish homes.

For more information, write or call:

Newport International Travel
2121 San Joaquin Hills Rd.
Newport Beach, CA 92660
Tel: 800-345-8444 (outside CA)
Tel: 949-719-2800
Fax: 949-719-2378
www.newportinternational.net/travel.html
engin@newportinternational.net

The agencies listed below offer a wide variety of general and specific interest tours, as do those already listed, but they do not as yet offer special, food-related tours. Do inquire, though, about their customized itineraries for independent travelers.

To My Turkey, Inc.
22356 Collington Dr.
Boca Raton, FL 33428
Tel: 866-988-7539
Fax: 561-892-4612
www.ToMyTurkey.com
info@ToMyTurkey.com

Glorious Adventures
10007 Gaynor Ave.
North Hills, CA 91343
Tel: 818-893-9030
Fax: 818-893-9151
gloradz@earthlink.net

Troy Tours
6151 W. Century Blvd., Suite 524
Los Angeles, CA 90045
Tel: 800-748-6878
Tel: 310-417-3460
Fax: 310-417-8849
www.troytours.com
info@troytours.com

Pacha Tours
226 5th Ave., 3rd FL
New York, NY 10001
Tel: 800-722-4288
Tel: 212-764-4080
Fax: 212-532-0635
www.pachatours.com
info@pachatours.com

Aegean Tours, Inc.
4306 Josephine Ave.
Beltsville, MD 20705
Tel: 301-937-8673
Fax: 301-937-1958
www.aegeantours.com
aegeantours@aegeantours.com

Far Horizons
PO Box 91900
Albuquerque, NM 87199
Tel: 800-552-4575
Fax: 505-343-8076
www.farhorizon.com
journey@farhorizon.com

Christopherson Travel
5588 S. Green St.
Salt Lake City, UT 84123
Tel: 866-327-7600
Fax: 801-327-7606

Fos Tours
51 Middle Ln., Suite 1
Jericho, NY 11753
Tel: 800-367-3450
Tel: 516-937-7757
Fax: 516-937-9037
www.fostours.com

Hellenic Adventures
2940 Harriet Ave.
Minneapolis, MN 55450
Tel: 800-851-6349
Tel. 612-827-0937
Fax: 612-827-0939
www.hellenicadventures.com
info@hellenicadventures.com

Patty's Places
1251 NW 195th St.
Seattle, WA 98177
Tel: 800-775-3861
Fax: 206-542-8113
www.pattysplaces.com
patty@pattysplaces.com

A.T.C. Anadolu Tours
420 Madison Ave., 10th FL
New York, NY 10017
Tel: 888-ANADOLU
Tel: 212-755-6515
Fax: 212-486-4014
www.atc-anadolu.com

Treasures of Turkey
PO Box 714
Edmonds, WA 98020
Tel: 800-572-0526
www.treasuresofturkey.com

Meditalya Travel
6354 Hollywood St.
Jupiter, FL 33458
Tel: 561-691-5032
Fax: 561-799-6030
www.meditalya.com
meditalya@meditalya.com

CTC Turkey
123 Donna Dr.
Hanover, MA 02339
Tel: 888-711-4500
Fax: 781-829-8743
www.ctcturkey.com
info@ctcturkey.com

Asia Minor Travel & Tours
6919 W. Broward Blvd., PMB 259
Plantation, FL 33317
Tel: 800-532-2938
Tel: 954-792-5511
Fax: 954-792-5300
www.asiaminortours.com
info@asiaminortours.com

Helpful Phrases

For Use in Restaurants and Food Markets

In the Restaurant

The following phrases in Turkish will assist you in ordering food, learning more about the dish you ordered, and determining what specialties of a region are available. Each phrase also is written phonetically to help with pronunciation. Syllables in capital letters are accented. For further insight into the language, read the comments on Turkish grammar in the introduction to the *Menu Guide* (p. 69).

DO YOU HAVE A MENU?

Menünüz var mı?
Meh-new-newz vahr muh?

MAY I SEE THE MENU, PLEASE?

Menüyü görebilir miyim, lütfen?
Meh-new-YEW gur-reh-bee-LEER mee-yeem, LEWT-fehn?

MAY WE ORDER A SAMPLER PLATE OF WHAT THE CHEF HAS MADE TODAY?

Şefin bugün yaptığı yemeklerden birer örnek getirir misiniz?
Sheh-FIN BEW-gewn yahp-tuh-UH yeh-mehk-lehr-DEHN bee-REHR ewr-NEHK geh-tee-REER mees-see-neez?

WHAT DO YOU RECOMMEND?

Ne tavsiye edersiniz?
Neh tahv-see-YEH eh-DEHR-see-neez?

HELPFUL PHRASES

DO YOU HAVE . . . ?
(ADD AN ITEM FROM THE *MENU GUIDE* OR THE *FOODS & FLAVORS GUIDE.*)

. . . var mı?
. . . vahr muh?

WHAT ARE YOUR "SPECIALS" FOR TODAY?

Bugünkü özel yemeğiniz nedir?
BOO-gewn-kew ur-ZEHL yeh-meh-yeen-EEZ NEH-deer?

DO YOU HAVE ANY SPECIAL REGIONAL DISHES?

Bu yöreye ait özel yemeğiniz var mı?
Boo yur-reh-YEH ah-EET ur-ZEHL yeh-meh-yee-NEEZ vahr muh?

IS THIS DISH SPICY?

Bu yemek baharatlı mı?
Boo yeh-MEHK bah-hah-raht-LUH muh?

I / WE WOULD LIKE TO ORDER . . .

. . . alabilir miyim / miyiz.
. . . ah-lah-bee-LEER mee-yeem / mee-yeez.

WHAT ARE THE INGREDIENTS IN THIS DISH?

Bu yemeğin içinde neler var?
Boo yeh-meh-YEEN eech-een-DEH neh-LEHR vahr?

WHAT ARE THE FLAVORINGS / SEASONINGS IN THIS DISH?

Bu yemeğe tat veren şeyler / baharatlar nelerdir?
Boo yeh-meh-YEH taht vehr-EHN sheh-LEHR / bah-hah-raht-LAHR neh-LEHR-deer?

THANK YOU VERY MUCH. THE FOOD WAS DELICIOUS.

Çok teşekkür ederim. Yemekleriniz enfes olmuş.
Chohk teh-shehk-KEWR eh-deh-reem. Yeh-mehk-lehr-een-EEZ ehn-FEHS ohl-MOOSH.

In the Market

The following phrases will help you make purchases and learn more about unfamiliar produce, spices and herbs.

WHAT SPECIAL VEGETABLES / FRUITS ARE GROWN LOCALLY?

Bu yöreye ait sebze ve meyvalarınız nelerdir?

Boo yur-reh-YEH ah-EET sehb-ZEH veh meh-vah-lahr-un-UZ neh-LEHR-deer?

WHAT IS THIS CALLED?

Bunun ismi nedir?

Boo-NOON ees-MEE NEH-deer?

DO YOU HAVE . . . ?
(ADD AN ITEM FROM THE *FOODS & FLAVORS GUIDE*.)

. . . var mı?

. . . vahr muh?

MAY I TASTE THIS?

Bunun tadına bakabilir miyim?

Boo-NOON tah-duh-NAH bah-kah-bee-LEER mee-yeem?

WHERE CAN I BUY FRESH . . . ?

Nerede taze . . . bulabilirim?

NEH-reh-deh tah-ZEH . . . boo-lah-bee-LEER-eem?

HOW MUCH IS THIS PER KILOGRAM?

Bunun kilosu kaç lira?

Boo-NOON kee-loh-SOO kahch lee-RAH?

I WOULD LIKE TO BUY . . . GRAMS OF THIS / THAT.

Bundan . . . gram veriniz.

Boon-DAHN . . . grahm VEHR-ee-neez.

WHERE CAN I WATCH . . . BEING MADE?

Nerede . . . yapılışını görebilirim?

NEH-reh-deh . . . yah-puh-luh-shu-NUH gur-reh-bee-LEER-eem?

MAY I PHOTOGRAPH THIS?

Bunun resmini çekebilir miyim?

Boo-NOON rehs-mee-NEE chehk-eh-bee-LEER mee-yeem?

Other Useful Phrases

Sometimes it helps to see in writing a word or phrase that is said to you in Turkish, because certain letters have distinctly different sounds in Turkish than in English. You may be familiar with the word and its English translation but less familiar with its pronunciation. The following phrase comes in handy if you want to see the word or phrase you are hearing.

PLEASE WRITE IT ON A PIECE
OF PAPER.

Lütfen bunu bir kağıda yazınız.
LEWT-fehn boo-NOO beer kah-yuh-DAH YAH-zuh-nuhz.

Interested in bringing home books about Turkish food? Perhaps some restaurateurs know just the place for you to look, if you pose the following question.

WHERE CAN I BUY A TURKISH
COOKBOOK IN ENGLISH?

İngilizce yazılmış Türk yemek kitabı nerede bulabilirim?
Een-gee-LEEZ-jeh yah-zuhl-MUHSH Tewrk yeh-MEHK kee-tah-BUH NEH-reh-deh boo-lah-bee-LEE-reem?

And, of course, the following phrases also are useful to know.

WHERE IS THE LADIES' / MEN'S
RESTROOM?

Bay / Bayan tuvaleti nerededir?
Beye / Beye-YAHN too-vah-leh-TEE NEH-reh-deh-deer?

MAY I HAVE THE CHECK,
PLEASE?

Lütfen hesabı getirir misiniz?
LEWT-fehn heh-sah-BUH geh-tee-REER mees-see-neez?

DO YOU ACCEPT CREDIT CARDS?
TRAVELERS CHECKS?

Banka kartı / Seyahat çeki kabul ediyor musunuz?
BAHN-kah kahr-TUH / Seh-yah-HAHT cheh-KEE kah-BOOL eh-DEE-yor moo-soo-nooz?

Menu Guide

This alphabetical listing is an extensive compilation of menu entries in Turkish, with English translations, to make food ordering easy. It includes typical Turkish fare as well as regional specialties.

Noteworthy, not-to-be-missed dishes with country-wide popularity are labeled "national favorite" in the margin next to the menu entry. Classic regional dishes of Turkey—also not to be missed—are labeled "regional classic." Note that outside a particular geographical area, with the possible exception of İstanbul, local specialties are unlikely to be found unless a restaurant features one or more regional cuisines. Comments on some of our favorites also are included in the margin.

With *Eat Smart in Turkey* in hand, you will quickly become more familiar with restaurant cuisine. Be sure to have it with you at breakfast in the hotel; there will be plenty of items to identify. Although Turks eat a light breakfast, the customary complimentary one in hotels often is an elaborate spread— fruits in season, fruit juices, cheeses, several varieties of olives, creamy, home-made yogurt, breads and rolls, cereals, cakes, eggs and cold cuts await you. Even the smaller establishments provide an adequate selection.

In hotel restaurants, breakfast, or *kahvaltı,* generally is served 7–10 AM. At non-tourist restaurants, however, breakfast is not commonly offered. Turks prefer to eat this meal at home, or to buy something at a *büfe,* a small snack shop or booth, on the way to work. Lunch, or *öğle yemeği,* is served from about 12–2 PM. The main meal of the day is dinner, or *akşam yemeği,* which is served from about 7–9 PM. In metropolitan areas, expect restaurants to stay open longer for dinner.

Some Helpful Language Insights for Menu Reading

For those interested in knowing more about interpreting the menu, it will be helpful to learn some basic features of the Turkish language, concentrating on Turkish nouns and their suffixes, since these are the words encountered most when dealing with food. Fortunately for us, the Turks replaced their Arabic alphabet in 1928 with our familar Latin one. Although used for centuries, the Arabic alphabet was poorly suited for spoken Turkish, and literacy suffered because it was hard to learn to write the sounds in Arabic. A few additional symbols such as umlauts and the unfamiliar undotted i (ı) were added to the the new Turkish alphabet to accommodate different vowel sounds. The circumflexed a, i and u (â, î, and û), present in a few words, generally lengthen the vowel sound; they are not of Turkish origin. Some consonants with diacritical marks such as ş, ç and the silent ğ, which lengthens the vowel preceding it, were added to the alphabet. The chapter *Helpful Phrases* (p. 65) offers tips on how to pronounce Turkish letters.

A basic characteristic of Turkish is the use of suffixes to modify the meaning of root words; several can be added. Among those for noun roots are the equivalents of prepositions and possessive adjectives—words that exist separately in English. Within each suffix category, there are at least two choices, equal in meaning, but the correct choice is dictated by the principle of vowel harmony.

To understand the significance of vowel harmony, it is necessary to know that Turkish vowels belong to one of two groups, depending on where in the mouth the sound is formed. The thin, fine (*ince*) vowels, eiöü, are formed in the front of the oral cavity; the thick, coarse (*kalın*) vowels, aıou, are formed in the back. For a Turkish root word to obey vowel harmony, its vowel sounds must be made in a similar way. To achieve this, a root must contain vowels from one group or the other, not from both, and its suffixes must contain vowels from this same group. Note, however, that some Turkish root words of foreign origin understandably do violate this principle of vowel harmony by having a mixture of vowels from both groups. Nevertheless, Turkish grammatical rules are applied to the suffixes of these borrowed words, and the terminal root vowel determines which vowel group is to be used for them.

An example of how suffixes obey vowel harmony is seen in the way nouns are pluralized. There are two derivative choices, *-ler* or *-lar*. For example, *sebze* means "vegetable." Its plural form must be *sebzeler* so that all vowels consistently are from the *ince* group, eiöü. *Balık* means fish. Its plural form is *balıklar* because its root vowels are from the *kalın* group, aıou. The few exceptions to pluralization in this manner occur with certain foreign roots, which obey the grammatical rules of the language of origin. For example, the word *bahar,* or spice, is Arabic, and it retains the Arabic plural form, *baharat.*

On menus, you will see that each section typically is headed by the plural form of the word for a particular category.

When there exists for each vowel group more than one choice of suffix within a given category, the following general rule applies:

	Terminal Root Vowel	Suffix Vowel
Group I	e or i	i
(*İnce*)	ö or ü	ü
Group II	a or ı	ı
(*Kalın*)	o or u	u

Menu readers will be interested in several other frequently encountered noun suffixes. To denote that something contains something else, meaning "with," the suffix choices are *-li, -lı, -lu* and *-lü.* Examples are as follows: the word for garlic is *sarımsak.* If garlic is a prominent ingredient in some dish, the word *sarımsaklı,* meaning "with garlic" may be included in the name of the dish to indicate this. *Et* means meat. If you want your soup broth to contain meat, look for the word *etli* in the name. To imply "without," the following suffix set is used: *-siz, -sız, -suz* and *-süz.*

To indicate ingredient or provenance, or "of," the suffixes *-i, -ı, -u* and *-ü* are used. Should the root word itself end in a vowel, a buffer letter "s," is added to the suffix to form *-si, -sı, -su -sü.* For example, *erik* means plum and *hoşaf* means compote. Therefore, *erik hoşafı* is a compote of plums. *Çorba* means soup and Adana is both a province in the Mediterranean region of Turkey and a city within it. Therefore, *Adana çorbası* is soup of Adana, a specialty of Adana province. Do recognize, however, that ending consonants of root words often change to a different, specific consonant when followed by a suffix vowel. Just when you think you recognize a familiar Turkish word like *kebap* on a menu, you'll see *kebabı* elsewhere, as in the dish *Adana kebabı.* This is because the final letter "p" of *kebap* must become "b" when the suffix "ı" is added to indicate that the preparation is a "*kebap* of something," in this case, of Adana. It is a spicy, minced meat mixture grilled on flat skewers, and it must be tried!

Though more useful in markets than restaurants, the following suffix will be handy to know if you want to find a particular vendor. To indicate that someone is a seller of something, the suffix choices are *-ci, -cı, -çi, -çı, -cu, -cü, -çu* and *-çü.* Thus a *baklavacı* sells baklava and a *sütçü* sells milk. The choice of consonants is determined by whether the last consonant is hard or soft.

Acem köftesi breaded and fried meatballs stuffed with a mixture of currants and pine nuts, Persian style.

Acem yahnisi ragout of chicken with walnuts and pomegranate juice, Persian style.

acıbadem kurabiyesi macaroon made with bitter almonds.

açma a type of puff pastry.

Adana çorbası a soup containing tomatoes, chickpeas and tiny meatballs, flavored with a touch of vinegar. It is a specialty of the province of Adana in the Mediterranean region of Turkey.

REGIONAL CLASSIC **Adana kebabı** spicy, flattened sausage-shaped kebabs of minced lamb, which are grilled on broad, flat skewers. They are served on top of pieces of *pide* bread and garnished with roasted tomatoes and peppers. A relish of thinly sliced onions, broad-leaf parsley and *sumak* typically accompanies this dish. It is a specialty of the province of Adana in the Mediterranean region of Turkey.

alamenda salata a salad of beets, potatoes and raw onions.

REGIONAL CLASSIC **Ali Nazik kebabı** purée of roasted eggplant mixed with yogurt and topped with a seasoned, minced lamb mixture. This dish is a variation of *hünkâr beğendi* (see this *Guide*).

Ali Paşa pilâvı buttered rice pilaf containing pine nuts and very small meatballs.

altın sarısı dil filetosu breaded fillet of sole.

Antep fıstığı ezmesi see *fıstık ezmesi.*

REGIONAL CLASSIC **Arabaşı çorbası** spicy tomato and chicken soup with red pepper paste. Regional variations include serving this dish with cold cubes of a cooked batter of flour and water to complement the piping hot, zesty soup.

Arap kadayıfı see *yassı kadayıf.*

Arap köftesi small balls or patties of a fried bulgur mixture, which was traditional food for travelers because it kept well.

NATIONAL FAVORITE **Arnavut ciğeri** an appetizer of fried lamb's liver, Albanian style, garnished with a relish of raw, sliced onion laced with chopped flat-leaf parsley and crushed red pepper. Usually served hot, it is one of the most popular appetizers enjoyed with *rakı,* Turkey's anise-flavored national liquor distilled from grapes. In fact, their tastes are considered so compatible that the liver is sometimes soaked in *rakı* before it is dredged in flour and fried.

REGIONAL CLASSIC **asma yaprağında sardalya** sardines baked in grape leaves.

aspurlu pilâv a safflower-flavored rice pilaf with minced meat; also called *haspirli pilâv.*

asude helva a type of halvah made with sugar, cornstarch, water and melted butter.

aşure a thick, sweet pudding of hulled whole wheat, legumes, nuts, and dried and fresh fruits. The preparation of this dessert, also called "Noah's Pudding," is a "thanksgiving" celebration of the meal of similar ingredients that Noah and his family are said to have concocted, using whatever food was left on the Ark when the flood waters receded. Making and eating this dish also commemorates the martyrdom of the grandson of the Prophet Mohammed. **NATIONAL FAVORITE**

avcı kebabı a dish of diced lamb, potatoes, carrots and peas.

ay çöreği crescent-shaped puff pastry filled with walnut paste.

ayran a popular and refreshing, lightly salted drink containing yogurt beaten with an equal amount of water, usually served with ice cubes. **REFRESHING**

ayva dolması quince stuffed with a mixture of rice and ground lamb, flavored with cinnamon, allspice and nutmeg.

ayva kompostosu a stewed quince compote.

ayva peltesi a gelatin-like paste of quince, cut into diamond-shaped pieces. **TASTY**

ayva reçeli quince jam.

ayva tatlısı quince stewed in syrup.

ayva yahnisi a ragout of lamb braised with quince. **NATIONAL FAVORITE**

baba tatlısı small, syrup-soaked cakes topped with thick cream called *kaymak* and ground pistachios.

badem çorbası a creamy soup with ground almonds.

badem şerbeti almond sherbet.

badem taratorlu levrek poached sea bass served with a ground almond sauce.

bademli kuru kayısı poached dried apricots, stuffed with chopped almonds and soaked in syrup. **DELICIOUS**

bademli muhallebi milk pudding with almonds.

bahçıvan çorbası a winter vegetable soup with minced lamb and homemade noodles.

bahçıvan kebabı lamb cooked with vegetables.

bahçıvan köftesi meatballs cooked with vegetables.

baklava any of several delicious, syrup-soaked confections made with layers of thin pastry dough called *yufka,* ground nuts and sometimes a thick cream called *kaymak.* **NATIONAL FAVORITE**

NATIONAL FAVORITE   **bal kabağı tatlısı** cooked, sugared pumpkin, mashed and topped with nuts and whipped cream.

balık çorbası fish soup.

DELICIOUS   **balık ekmek** a fried fish sandwich.

balık köftesi fish balls.

balık pastırması smoked and dried fish.

ballı tavuk chicken with honey sauce.

REGIONAL CLASSIC   **bamya çorbası** okra soup.

bamyalı tavuk chicken with okra.

barbunya pilâki a cold salad of red beans stewed in olive oil.

bastı a vegetable stew.

batırık a cold salad of bulgur and ground walnuts mixed with tomatoes and herbs and formed into oblong patties.

beğendi see *hünkâr beğendi.*

beğendili incik kebap leg of lamb with eggplant purée.

beğendili piliç chicken with eggplant purée.

beyaz peynir ezmesi white cheese dip.

GREAT CHOICE   **beyaz peynirli yumurta** eggs cooked in a bed of melted white cheese.

beyaz şarap soslu levrek sea bass in white wine sauce.

beyin haşlaması boiled brain.

beyin kızartması fried brain.

beyinli pilâv pilaf with brain.

Beykoz kebabı pieces of lamb wrapped in lengthwise slices of eggplant, topped with tomato slices and baked in tomato sauce, a specialty of Beykoz, a neighborhood of İstanbul on the Asian side of the Bosphorus.

REGIONAL CLASSIC   **Beykoz usülü paça** trotters cooked in the style of Beykoz, a neighborhood of İstanbul on the Asian side of the Bosphorus. Boiled sheep's trotters cooked in garlic and olive oil are served on a slice of fried bread and covered with egg yolk and lemon sauce.

bıldırcın ızgara grilled quail.

bıldırcınlı pilâv pilaf with quail.

biber salçası red pepper paste made from sun-dried sweet red peppers. Hot pastes are a mixture of sweet and hot peppers.

Bitlis köftesi balls of minced lamb and bulgur stuffed with a mixture of rice and pomegranate seeds; a specialty of Bitlis, a province in eastern Turkey.

REGIONAL CLASSIC   **bohça böreği** a *börek* filled with minced lamb. It is named for the way the layers of dough are bundled around the filling.

borani Persian-style spinach stew with rice and yogurt.

bostana tomato and green pepper salad.

boza popular winter drink made of fermented millet, traditionally   NATIONAL FAVORITE
sprinkled on top with cinnamon and roasted chickpeas.

buğu kebabı steamed lamb with tomatoes, onion and garlic.

Buhara pilâvı pilaf with lamb, carrots and almonds; a preparation
attributed to Bukhara, a city in Uzbekistan.

bulgur pilâvı pilaf made with bulgur.

bulgurlu mercimekli köfte a cold salad of cooked bulgur and   FLAVORFUL
lentils formed into patties.

bumbar dolması intestines stuffed with a mixture of lamb's or
sheep's lung and rice.

burma pistachio-stuffed coils made from thin sheets of pastry
dough called *yufka,* which are baked and and soaked in syrup.

Bursa kebabı slices of *döner kebabı* placed on top of fresh *pide*   REGIONAL CLASSIC
bread that has been spread with tomato sauce and covered with
whipped yogurt. Browned butter is then drizzled over
everything. This dish is a specialty of Bursa, a city in the Sea of
Marmara region of Turkey. It is also called *İskender kebabı,*
after a famous kebab restaurant in Bursa.

Bursa tavuğu chicken in cream sauce with capers and olives, a
specialty of Bursa, a city in the Sea of Marmara region of Turkey.

bülbül yuvası (nightingale's nest) a nest-shaped dessert made   NATIONAL FAVORITE
with nuts and a few layers of thin pastry dough called *yufka,*
which are rolled like a jelly roll on a thin rolling pin, or *oklava.*
This pastry roll is then tightly compressed into a puckered ring
by pushing it from both ends towards the center, then removed
to a baking pan. The nests are baked, filled with chopped
pistachios and soaked in sugar syrup.

büryan pilâvı a casserole of lamb and tomatoes baked on top of rice.

cacık a popular dill- or mint-flavored salad of yogurt, grated   NATIONAL FAVORITE
cucumber and garlic. It is also enjoyed as a cold soup by adding
water or a few ice cubes.

cevizli baklava baklava made with walnuts.

cevizli beyaz peynir white cheese and walnut dip.

cevizli biber a paste of ground walnuts, mashed red pepper and   REGIONAL CLASSIC
onions, spiked with hot red pepper to taste.

cevizli çörek a square of rich, flaky pastry filled with a ground walnut mixture. The ends of the dough are tucked underneath, like flaps of an envelope.

cevizli patlıcan salatası a salad of puréed eggplant and chopped walnuts.

cevizli tarator a sauce of ground walnuts, garlic, olive oil and vinegar, which is eaten especially with fried mussels.

REGIONAL CLASSIC   **cevizli tulum peyniri** an appetizer of walnuts mixed with *tulum,* an aged, salty cheese.

EXCELLENT CHOICE   **cızbız köfte** grilled balls of minced lamb, flavored with cumin; also called *kimyonlu sahan köftesi.*

ciğer kebabı liver kebab.

ciğer kızartması fried liver.

ciğer pane breaded and fried liver.

ciğer sarma minced lamb liver and lung wrapped in caul, or omentum, which is part of the abdominal lining, and baked. To aficionados of the Scottish *haggis,* this is a reasonable facsimile.

cizleme a yeast pancake.

çatal aşı hulled whole wheat, lentil and red bean soup, thick enough to be eaten with a fork.

çatı böreği a type of turnover made with cheese.

Çerkes çorbası creamy soup containing small pieces of chicken-filled pasta; a preparation attributed to the Circassians.

Çerkes puf böreği small turnovers made of thin pastry dough called *yufka,* which are filled with a goat's milk cheese and deep-fried; a preparation attributed to the Circassians.

NATIONAL FAVORITE   **Çerkes tavuğu** a cold appetizer of shredded chicken in a pulverized walnut sauce and topped with paprika-flavored walnut oil, a preparation attributed to the Circassians.

NATIONAL FAVORITE   **çılbır** poached eggs served in warmed yogurt and drizzled with melted butter containing hot red pepper flakes.

çıplak börek a *börek* made with squash, eggs, flour and parsley, and baked. It is cut into wedges and served. This dish is similar to the fritter called *mücver.*

REGIONAL CLASSIC   **çiğ köfte** oblong pieces of raw, minced lamb kneaded with finely ground bulgur and seasoned with green onions, flat-leaf parsley, hot red pepper and cumin. The pieces should retain the shallow impressions made by the fingers when being formed. Since this is a dish made with uncooked meat, be discriminating where you order it.

çikolatalı ay chocolate, crescent-shaped cookies.

çinakop ızgara a young *lüfer* fish, grilled.

çoban salatası a mint-flavored salad of coarsely chopped tomatoes, peppers, cucumbers and onions in an oil and lemon juice dressing.

çökelek salata a salad made with soft cheese curds from skim milk, tomatoes, onions and parsley in a vinaigrette sauce.

çömlek kebabı lamb and vegetables baked in an earthenware pot, sometimes over hot embers.

çöp kebabı see *çöp şiş.*

çöp şiş small cubes of lamb grilled on wooden skewers. This dish is also called *çöp kebabı.*

çulluk kızartması roasted woodcock.

damat dolması scooped-out shells of summer squash stuffed with a mixture of squash, minced lamb and nuts, and garnished with garlic and yogurt sauce.

dana etli makarana macaroni with veal.

dana etli tas kebabı *tas kebabı* made with veal.

dana göğsü dolması stuffed veal breast.

dana rosto pounded veal flank steak marinated in milk and olive oil, rolled like a jelly roll and simmered. It is sliced and served cold.

dilber dudağı (beauty's lips) a pastry made from two small balls of dough pressed together and shaped to look like lips. It is fried in oil and soaked in syrup.

dolama a dessert made with layers of thin pastry dough called *yufka,* filled with a paste of pistachios and rolled up like a jelly roll. Also called *dürüm.*

domates dolması stuffed tomatoes.

domates salçalı köfte balls of minced lamb cooked in tomato sauce.

domates salçası tomato paste made from sun-dried tomato pulp.

domates soslu kebap flattened, sausage-shaped kebabs made of spicy minced lamb, placed on top of eggplant slices and covered with roasted tomato and pepper sauce.

domatesli bulgurlu piliç chicken with bulgur and tomatoes.

domatesli dil balığı flounder cooked with tomatoes.

domatesli kaz yahnisi ragout of goose with tomatoes.

domatesli mercimek çorbası red lentil and tomato soup.

domatesli patlıcan tavası a cold appetizer of fried eggplant in tomato and garlic sauce.

domatesli pilâv tomato pilaf.

domatesli pirinç çorbası tomato and rice soup.

döğmeli alaca çorba a soup with lamb, hulled whole wheat, or *dövme*, fresh red bell pepper, chickpeas and onion, flavored with tarragon.

NATIONAL FAVORITE döner kebabı thin slices of lamb cut from a large, wedge-shaped slab of meat roasted on an upright, slowly revolving spit. The slab is a composite of many thick slices of meat layered together, with the larger slices on top. Roasted peppers and tomatoes traditionally accompany this lamb kebab; sometimes bulgur or rice also is included.

döner üstü pilâv slices of lamb roasted on an upright spit and served on top of rice; compare with *döner kebabı.*

NATIONAL FAVORITE düğün çorbası a soup with finely diced lamb, thickened with butter and flour, and flavored with beaten egg yolk and lemon sauce. A butter and paprika mixture is drizzled on the surface.

dürüm a long piece of dough several inches wide covered with chunks of meat or liver and vegetables and rolled like a jelly roll. Also the name for a rolled dessert (see *dolama*).

ekmek dolması thick-crusted round bread hollowed out and filled with a mixture of minced lamb and bread crumbs. The stuffed bread is then simmered in broth.

NATIONAL FAVORITE ekmek kadayıfı a dessert made from special bread dough, which is pre-soaked in hot water to soften and swell it, and then baked in sugar syrup. Pieces often are cut in two and filled with a thick, rich cream called *kaymak.*

ekşi aşı a somewhat sour, yogurt-based soup with rice, chickpeas, herbs and small, sausage-shaped pieces of minced meat encased in a bulgur coating.

ekşili köfte meatballs in an egg yolk and lemon sauce.

REGIONAL CLASSIC ekşili ufak köfte small balls of minced lamb and bulgur in a spicy tomato sauce flavored with lemon. Compare with *ufak köfte* and *yuvarlama.*

Elbasan tavası a casserole of lamb with yogurt sauce attributed to a region in Albania.

elmalı börek apple pastry made with thin dough called *yufka.*

enginar orturma a casserole of artichoke hearts covered with minced meat and topped with tomato halves.

erik marmelâtı plum marmelade.

erişte a dish of homemade noodles.

et mangal see *mangalda et.*

et suyu consommé.

etli biber dolması green pepper stuffed with a seasoned minced   NATIONAL FAVORITE
meat mixture.

etli çalı fasulyesi a stew of green beans and meat.

etli ekmek see *etli pide.*

etli enginar dolması artichokes stuffed with a minced lamb mixture.

etli güveç a casserole of meat with a variety of vegetables.

etli ıspanak a meat and spinach dish.

etli kara lâhana sarma a minced meat mixture wrapped in black   REGIONAL CLASSIC
cabbage leaves.

etli kuru fasulye a stew of white kidney beans and lamb with
tomatoes, potatoes and carrots.

etli lâhana dolması cabbage stuffed with a minced meat and
rice mixture.

etli nohut chickpeas with meat.

etli pide a pizza-like preparation made with long, thin *pide* bread   REGIONAL CLASSIC
covered with minced lamb, three varieties of grated cheese
(*kaşar, tulum* and *beyaz peynir*) and green pepper; a
specialty of Konya, a city in south-central Anatolia. Also called
etli ekmek.

etli soğan dolması onions stuffed with a meat mixture.

etli yeşil fasulye green beans with lamb.

ezme an appetizer and a relish made of finely chopped tomato,   EXTRAORDINARY
cucumber, pepper, hot pepper, onion and flat-leaf parsley in
olive oil and a touch of vinegar. Also called *ezme salatası.*

ezme salatası see *ezme.*

ezogelin çorbası red lentil soup with bulgar or rice, flavored with   NATIONAL FAVORITE
mint, and often served with lemon juice on the side.

fasulye ezmesi a salad made with mashed beans.

fasulye pilâkisi a cold dish of white beans stewed in olive oil with
carrots, potatoes, celery root and onion.

fasulye piyazı a cold, marinated white bean salad.

fasulye yaprağı dolması, Malatya usülü green bean leaves stuffed   REGIONAL CLASSIC
with a hulled wheat and bulgur mixture, simmered in yogurt
sauce and served topped with sautéed onions, in the style of
Malatya, a city in central Anatolia.

fındıklı baklava baklava made with hazelnuts.

REGIONAL CLASSIC **fırın kebabı** generous portions of oven-roasted lamb served with pieces of *pide* bread; a specialty of Konya, a city in central Anatolia.

fırın makarna baked macaroni.

NATIONAL FAVORITE **fırın sütlâç** rice pudding topped with beaten egg yolk, and baked until a brown crust forms; compare with the unbaked version called *sütlâç*.

fırında ispendik baked small (young) bass.

fırında kuzu budu roast leg of lamb.

REGIONAL CLASSIC **fırında lüfer** baked *lüfer,* a fish similar to the bluefish (see *Foods & Flavors Guide*).

fırında piliç kızartması chicken fried in oil and oven-roasted.

fırında yumurta baked eggs.

WONDERFUL **fıstık ezmesi** a fantastic and colorful dessert made of pistachios and sugar, which is boiled, kneaded and formed into rolls. It is also called Antep *fıstığı ezmesi* because it is a specialty of the southeastern city Antep, now Gaziantep, the pistachio capital of Turkey.

fıstıklı künefe a pistachio-containing variation of the dessert *künefe;* see *künefe.*

fıstıklı muhallebi milk pudding with rice and ground pistachios.

fıstıklı patlıcanlı pilâv pilaf with eggplant and pine nuts.

fıstıklı revani a cake made with semolina and finely ground pistachios, which is typically served with the rich, thick cream called *kaymak.*

göbete böreği a *börek* filled with minced lamb, tomatoes, green peppers and garlic.

NATIONAL FAVORITE **gözleme** thin circles of rolled dough covered with meat, cheese or vegetables, which are folded like an envelope and griddle-fried.

gül reçeli a preserve flavored with rose petals.

gül sulu muhallebi milk pudding flavored with rose-petal extract.

gül suyu katılmış sütlâç rice pudding flavored with rose-petal extract.

gül şerbeti sherbet flavored with rose-petal extract.

gül şurubu a syrup made from rose-petal extract, which is diluted with water and ice to make a drink.

gülbe şekeri şemsiyesi a sweet of sugar and rose-petal extract.

TOP A garlic seller in the old marketplace *(Uzun Çarşı)* in Antakya. **ABOVE LEFT** Taking a tea break in a tea garden *(çay bahçesi)* near the Egyptian Spice Market *(Mısır Çarşısı)* in İstanbul. The New Mosque *(Yeni Cami)* is in the background. **ABOVE RIGHT** A menu in the doorway of a restaurant in Marmaris, notifying potential customers of the good Turkish home cooking available within.

TOP LEFT Baking mountains of *pide* bread in Gaziantep. **TOP RIGHT** A young man offering *şerbet*, a refreshing cold drink, usually fruit-based, from the metal container on his back. By tradition, a *şerbet* seller (*şerbetçi*) clicks together two metal saucers to call attention to his wares. **BOTTOM** *Havuç baklava* made by the Güllü brothers in Gaziantep. The Güllü family has been making such sinful sweetmeats for five generations at the famous Güllüoğlu confectionary.

TOP Munching fresh chickpeas *(nohut)* on the grounds of the hilltop citadel *(Hisar)* in Ankara. **MIDDLE** A tempting mound of fresh mulberries *(dut)* in one of Ankara's weekly outdoor markets *(Küçükesat Pazarı).* **BOTTOM** An outdoor vegetable and fruit market in Antalya.

TOP LEFT Ali Murat, head chef at İstanbul's Tuğra Restaurant, demonstrating the art of making eggplant kebabs *(patlıcan kebabı)*. Pieces of eggplant alternate with patties of minced chicken. **TOP RIGHT** A slab of lamb *(döner kebabı)*, a composite of thick slices of meat, roasting on a vertical spit at Arzum Döner, one of many kebab shops on the "street of kebabs" in Antalya. **ABOVE** Spice bins in the outdoor vegetable and fruit market in Antalya.

TOP LEFT A cherry seller in the outdoor market in Safranbolu. **TOP RIGHT** A young boy in İstanbul selling Turkey's most popular street snack, a twisted, ring-shaped roll *(simit)* coated with sesame seeds. Also artfully arranged on the pile are braided loaves of bread. **BOTTOM** Lustrous eggplant *(patlıcan),* Turkey's favorite vegetable, in the outdoor market in Marmaris.

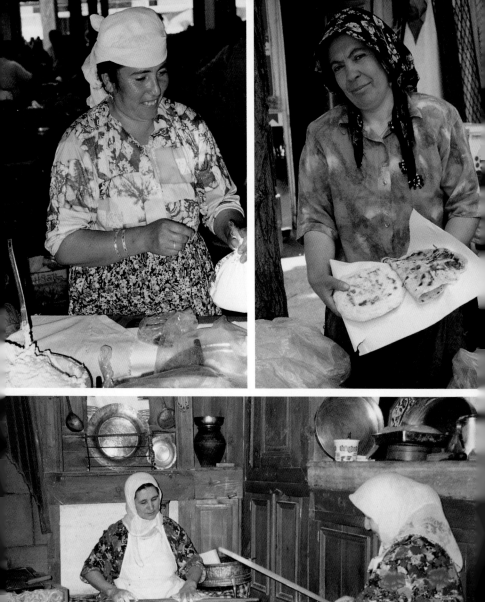

TOP LEFT Selling village yogurt in the weekly outdoor market in Marmaris. **TOP RIGHT** Griddle-baked breads for sale in one of Ankara's weekly outdoor markets *(Küçükesat Pazarı)*. *Bazlama* (left) is an unleavened circle about 1-inch thick. *Gözleme* is a thin circle of rolled dough usually filled with various mixtures, then folded and fried. **BOTTOM** Women sitting at low tables *(hamur açma sofrası)* rolling dough with long, narrow rolling pins *(oklava)*. Their creations will be served at the Zenger Paşa Konağı Restaurant in Ankara.

TOP LEFT An ice cream seller demonstrating the remarkable elastic quality of his ice cream *(dondurma)*. This celebrated recipe from Kahramanmaraş contains powdered orchid root *(sahleb)*, which gives the ice cream its taffy-like property. **TOP RIGHT** Brewing Turkish coffee in a long-handled, wide-necked pot *(cezve)*. **BOTTOM** *Mantı*, one of the oldest items on the Turkish menu, is attributed to the Chinese. These tiny meat- or cheese-filled pastas are served in a garlic and yogurt sauce.

TOP *Kaymaklı kayısı tatlısı,* a popular dessert of poached apricots stuffed with a rich, thick cream *(kaymak).* **MIDDLE** *İmam bayıldı,* or "the priest fainted," a beloved Ottoman dish of stuffed eggplant stewed in olive oil. **BOTTOM** *Adana kebabı,* spicy kebabs of minced meat grilled on broad, flat skewers. This preparation, a specialty of the province of Adana, traditionally is served with roasted peppers and tomatoes, and a relish of sliced onions, flat-leaf parsley and *sumak,* a spice made from the berries of an edible variety of sumac shrub.

güllâç a silky, rose-flavored dessert made of finely ground nuts and thin rice wafers soaked in milk, and garnished with pomegranate seeds. NATIONAL FAVORITE

güneşte kayısı reçeli jam made from stewed apricots, which are thickened in the sun.

günün çorbası soup of the day.

güveç kebabı a lamb, tomato and onion stew cooked in individual-sized earthenware casseroles, whose lids are sealed with a thin strip of dough. REGIONAL CLASSIC

güveçte deniz mahsulleri a seafood casserole.

Halep işi kebap a spicy kebab with green peppers and parsley, served on pieces of *pide* bread; a preparation attributed to the Syrian city of Aleppo.

hamsi an anchovy-like fish popular in the Black Sea region.

hamsi buğulama poached *hamsi*.

hamsi çorbası *hamsi* soup.

hamsi kızartması fried *hamsi*.

hamsi köftesi fried balls made of chopped *hamsi* and liver, cornmeal and spices.

hamsi kuşu a pair of filleted *hamsi* cleverly wrapped around a filling of rice and pine nuts, dipped in cornmeal and beaten egg, and fried.

hamsi tavası breaded and fried *hamsi*. REGIONAL CLASSIC

hamsili börek a *börek* filled with a mixture of chopped *hamsi* and onion.

hamsili pilâv rice pilaf covered with a layer of fresh, filleted *hamsi* and baked. It is made like an upside-down cake and inverted prior to serving.

hamur çorbası a soup with homemade noodles.

hanım göbeği (lady's navel) a small, round pastry with a central depression, fried in oil and soaked in syrup. Also called *kadın göbeği*. NATIONAL FAVORITE

hanım güveci a braised lamb and vegetable casserole topped with puréed potatoes containing grated coconut.

hanım parmağı (lady's finger) a fried, finger-shaped appetizer made with minced beef.

hardallı kuzu böbreği lamb kidney in mustard.

Hasan Paşa kâğıt kebabı a dish of lamb and vegetables cooked in parchment paper.

Hasan Paşa köftesi minced lamb patties with a dollop of mashed potatoes in the center.

haspirli pilâv see *aspurlu pilâv.*

haşhaşlı nokul poppyseed roll.

haşlama sığır eti stewed beef.

havuç baklava baklava made in a round pan with thin layers of pastry dough called *yufka,* and chopped nuts. It typically is cut into narrow wedges, which are carrot-shaped, not carrot-containing.

havuç kızartması fried carrots.

havuç salatası carrot salad.

havuçlu gözleme a thin circle of rolled dough sprinkled with grated carrots, onions and parsley, folded in four places to make an envelope and griddle-fried.

haydari an appetizer of yogurt mixed with sheep's cheese and olive oil to make a paste, and flavored with mint and paprika.

helva any of several halvah desserts made with semolina, sesame paste or flour, mixed with sugar, nuts and flavorings.

hibeş an appetizer made of yogurt, chickpeas, red pepper and onion, spread on *pide* bread.

Hind tavuğu chicken curry, a dish of Indian origin.

hindi dolması stuffed turkey.

hindi suyuyla nohutlu bulgur pilâvı bulgur and chickpea pilaf simmered in turkey broth.

hindiba salatası a salad made with chicory or dandelion greens.

Hindistan cevizli muhallebi coconut pudding.

hoşmerim a dessert made with flour, fresh unsalted cheese or cream, and topped with honey or sugar.

humus a purée of chickpeas mixed with sesame oil, lemon juice, garlic, red pepper and spices.

hünkâr beğendi (sultan's delight) a purée of roasted eggplant with cream and grated cheese, topped with sautéed cubes of lamb in tomato sauce. Also called simply *beğendi.*

ıspanak bastısı spinach with rice.

ıspanak kökü salatası spinach root salad.

ıspanaklı tepsi böreği a *börek* with spinach filling, cooked in a tray.

ıspanaklı yumurta fried egg with spinach.

ızgara bulgurlu köfte grilled balls made of a spicy mixture of ground lamb and bulgur.

ızgara köfte grilled meatballs.   NATIONAL FAVORITE

ızgara patlıcan ve biber salatası a cold salad of minced, roasted eggplant and diced green peppers.

iç pilâv rice pilaf with dried currants, pine nuts and diced liver.   NATIONAL FAVORITE

içi yumurtalı köfte meatballs stuffed with hard-boiled eggs.

içli köfte oblong, tapered patties of minced lamb and bulgur,   REGIONAL CLASSIC
poked with a finger to make an opening, and filled with a minced meat, spice and nut mixture, sometimes containing rice. They can be boiled or fried. Compare with *sini köftesi.* Also called *kubbe.*

imam bayıldı (the priest fainted) a cold dish of eggplant stuffed   NATIONAL FAVORITE
with chopped tomatoes, onions, flat-leaf parsley and whole garlic cloves, and cooked in olive oil. Several explanations exist to account for the name of this dish, Turkey's best-known eggplant preparation. Equally plausible reasons for why "the priest fainted" upon eating this food are its exquisite taste and the copious amount of olive oil called for in its preparation.

incik yahnisi lamb shank stew.

incir dolması stewed figs filled with sugar and nuts and served with a rich, thick cream called *kaymak.*

incir reçeli fig jam.

İnegöl köftesi grilled meatballs containing semolina; a specialty   REGIONAL CLASSIC
of İnegöl, a city in the Sea of Marmara region of Turkey

irmik çorbası chicken broth with beaten eggs, milk, semolina and tomatoes.

irmik helvası halvah made with semolina and nuts, and flavored with saffron.

İskender kebabı see *Bursa kebabı*

islim kebabı a steamed kebab of lamb wrapped in lengthwise slices of eggplant.

İstanbul pilâvı buttered rice pilaf with almonds, pistachios, saffron and shredded chicken; a specialty of İstanbul.

istridye fırında baked oysters.

işkembe çorbası tripe soup.   NATIONAL FAVORITE

İzmir köftesi sausage-shaped pieces of a minced lamb mixture in   REGIONAL CLASSIC
tomato sauce; a specialty of the city of İzmir in the Aegean region of Turkey.

jelâtinli tavuk chicken with aspic.

DELICIOUS   **kabak böreği** a *börek* made with about a dozen layers of thin pastry dough called *yufka,* each brushed with a yogurt, butter and egg mixture and then stacked on top of each other. A filling of shredded zucchini seasoned with dill and flat-leaf parsley is placed on the middle layer of the stack.

kabak çiçeği dolması squash blossoms stuffed with a mixture of rice and pine nuts, and sometimes minced meat.

TASTY   **kabak kalye** zucchini rounds cooked with minced meat, tomatoes and green peppers, seasoned with fresh dill and mint.

REGIONAL CLASSIC   **kabak kış böreği** a pumpkin-filled *börek* rolled like a jelly roll. It is baked after several individual rolls are placed end to end in a round pan to form a coil.

kabak kızartması fried zucchini.

kabak musakkası layered slices of zucchini, topped with seasoned minced lamb and baked.

kabak mücveri fritters made with zucchini and *kaşar* cheese.

kabartma a fried, egg-coated slice of bread, dusted with powdered sugar.

kaburga dolması lamb ribs stuffed with a mixture of minced kidney, liver, rice, pine nuts and currants.

kadayıf a syrup-soaked dessert made with commercially available pastry dough as a basis, which is either thread-like *(tel kadayıf),* flat or pancake-like *(yassı kadayıf)* or bread-like *(ekmek kadayıfı).* See individual dessert entries, this *Guide.*

NATIONAL FAVORITE   **kadın budu köfte (lady's thigh meatballs)** minced lamb mixed with cooked rice and formed into oval shapes resembling thighs, which are coated in egg and deep-fried.

kadın göbeği see *hanım göbeği.*

kalamar tava an appetizer of batter-coated, deep-fried squid.

kalkan tava fried turbot.

GREAT   **kalkan yumurtası tava** fried turbot roe.

kalye stewed marrow.

REGIONAL CLASSIC   **Kanlıca yoğurdu** a slice of thick, creamy yogurt served with powdered sugar on the side; a specialty of Kanlıca, a small town on the Asian coast of the Bosphorus.

NATIONAL FAVORITE   **kapama** pieces of spring lamb with bones, cooked with romaine lettuce leaves. Also called *kuzu kapama.*

kapuska a spicy winter stew of cabbage with lamb and peppers. It is called *kıymalı kapuska* when the meat is minced.

kara lâhana çorbası a soup made with black cabbage leaves; a speciality of the Black Sea region.

karagöz buğulama steamed sea bream.

karışık ızgara mixed grill.

karışık komposto mixed compote, made with assorted large fresh fruits.

karides Halikarnas shrimp simmered in wine and tomatoes, sprinkled with grated cheese; a specialty of the city of Bodrum on the Mediterranean, the site of ancient Halicarnassus.

karides şiş shrimp grilled on a skewer.

karnıbahar musakka a casserole of cauliflower florets topped with seasoned, minced lamb and baked.

karnıyarık eggplant, slit and stuffed with minced meat, tomatoes and peppers.

kaşarlı köfte meatballs with *kaşar* cheese.

katmer a flaky pastry made with twisted strips of dough filled with a paste of crushed pistachios and the thick, rich cream called *kaymak*.

kavun dolması a hollowed-out melon stuffed with melon balls and other fruits.

kavurma lamb fried on a convex griddle, or *saç*. This is a common method of cooking lamb following its sacrifice for religious purposes. In the past, this fried meat was salted and preserved for winter; also called *saç kavurma*.

kaygana a crêpe-like dessert made with eggs and served with powdered sugar.

kayısı pestili sheets of dried apricots made of sun-dried fruit pastes.

kayısılı dondurma apricot ice cream.

kaymak helvası halvah made with semolina and the thick, rich cream called *kaymak*.

kaymaklı elma kompostosu a compote of stewed apples topped with the thick, rich cream called *kaymak*.

kaymaklı kayısı tatlısı dried apricots, poached and filled with either the thick, rich cream called *kaymak* or a yogurt cream, garnished with grated pistachios and served chilled. Also called *kaymaklı kuru kayısı*.

kaymaklı kuru kayısı see *kaymaklı kayısı tatlısı*.

Kayseri köftesi cumin-seasoned patties of minced lamb covered with sliced tomatoes are baked on top of sliced potatoes; a preparation associated with the city of Kayseri in central Anatolia.

NATIONAL FAVORITE **kazan dibi (bottom of the kettle)** a firm, milk and rice flour pudding, rolled like a jelly roll, with a dark brown surface. To obtain this shape and coloration, the pudding is baked in a shallow pan and then placed over a burner to brown the bottom. When cool and set, rectangular pieces are cut from the pan and rolled up with the browned bottom outside. Historically, this dessert was the burned remnants stuck to the bottom of the pot when making the puddings *tavuk göğsü*, which contains finely shredded chicken breast, and *muhallebi*. When *kazan dibi* also contains chicken, it is called *tavuk göğsü kazan dibi*. See *tavuk göğsü*.

kâğıtta barbunya red mullet baked in parchment paper.

kâğıtta kebap lamb and vegetables baked in parchment paper.

kâğıtta kefal balığı gray mullet baked in parchment paper.

kâğıtta levrek sea bass fillets baked in parchment paper.

kefal pilâkisi a cold dish of gray mullet cooked in olive oil and onions.

kekikli salata salad seasoned with thyme.

REGIONAL CLASSIC **kelle paça** a stew containing sheep's trotters, tripe and head meat, a popular dish in the southeastern city of Gaziantep. This stew is typically consumed early in the morning, before breakfast, and is thought to provide great strength for the day.

kesme çorbası a soup containing flat, homemade noodles and green lentils; also called *tutmaç aşı*.

REGIONAL CLASSIC **kestane şekeri** chestnut glacé, a delicious specialty of Bursa; a city in the Sea of Marmara region of Turkey.

kestaneli dolma cabbage leaves stuffed with a mixture of chestnuts and rice.

kestaneli hindi güveci turkey casserole with chestnuts.

kestaneli pilâv rice pilaf with chestnuts.

kestaneli yahni lamb chops with chestnuts, glazed with molasses.

REGIONAL CLASSIC **keşkek** a dish of boiled, shredded lamb and hulled whole wheat called *dövme,* which are combined and beaten to make a paste.

NATIONAL FAVORITE **keşkül** an almond-flavored milk and rice custard. Preparations may contain pulverized almonds or have them strained from the mixture, leaving only the flavor. Also called *keşkülü fukara.*

REGIONAL CLASSIC **kete** a pastry filled with browned rice flour.

kılıç balığı ızgarası grilled swordfish.

kılıç şiş swordfish marinated in lemon juice and olive oil, and broiled on skewers.

kırma tavuk kebabı boneless chicken, split in two, and grilled.

kırmızı biberli piliç chicken with red pepper.

kırmızı mercimek çorbası red lentil soup.

kırmızı ve yeşil biber dolması stuffed red and green peppers.

kısır a cold salad of finely ground bulgur, chopped tomatoes and parsley mixed with olive oil and given a light tart taste with pomegranate or lemon juice. NATIONAL FAVORITE

kış türlüsü a casserole made with meat and winter vegetables, such as carrots, onions and potatoes. NATIONAL FAVORITE

kıymalı börek a *börek* filled with minced lamb, onion and butter, rolled like a jelly roll and formed into a crescent shape.

kıymalı ıspanak spinach with minced meat. NATIONAL FAVORITE

kıymalı kapuska see *kapuska*.

kıymalı makarna macaroni with minced meat.

kıymalı pırasa leeks with minced meat.

kıymalı yumurta eggs with minced meat.

kimyonlu sahan köftesi see *cızbız köfte*.

kiremit kebabı minced lamb patties cooked on a clay tile. REGIONAL CLASSIC

kiremitte balık fish baked on a clay tile.

kokoreç spit-roasted, stuffed lamb intestines.

koruk salatası a salad with a piquant dressing of minced tomatoes, garlic, herbs and the juice of unripe grapes.

koyun kolu sarma pounded mutton shoulder meat wrapped around carrots.

koyun yahnisi mutton ragout.

köfte çorbası meatball soup.

kömürde piliç charcoal-grilled chicken.

köylü çorbası a chicken and winter vegetable soup.

kremalı ıspanaklı yumurta eggs with spinach in a cream sauce. DELICIOUS

kremalı kebap kebabs in a cream sauce.

kremalı piliç chicken in a cream sauce.

kubbe see *içli köfte*.

kuru bakla ezmesi cold dish of mashed fava beans.

kuru baklava a variety of baklava prepared with less syrup than usual so that it keeps well for several weeks.

kuru erik hoşafı prune compote.

kuru fasulye stew made with dried white beans and lamb.

kuru incir tatlısı dried figs, poached and stuffed with ground walnuts.

kuru köfte finger-shaped meatballs dredged in flour and fried. They are quite dense and dry.

kuskus pilâvı couscous pilaf.

kuzu böbreği şişte lamb kidney shish kebab.

kuzu budu rostosu roast leg of lamb.

kuzu ciğeri yahnisi a ragout of lamb's liver.

kuzu Elbasan tava lamb with egg and yogurt sauce; a dish attributed to a region in Albania.

kuzu fırın oven-baked lamb.

GREAT CHOICE **kuzu güveci** lamb casserole.

kuzu haşlama boiled chunks of lamb, potatoes, carrots and celery root in an egg yolk and lemon sauce.

kuzu kapama see *kapama.*

kuzu pirzolası grilled lamb chops marinated in olive oil, onion and thyme.

kuzu pirzolası pane pounded lamb chops, breaded and fried.

kuzulu pilâv pilaf with lamb.

küçük yağlı simit small *mahleb*-flavored, ring-shaped rolls coated with beaten eggs and sesame seeds. They are harder than the standard *simit* sold on the streets.

REGIONAL CLASSIC **külbastı** grilled lamb cutlets with *çemen,* a paste made primarily of red pepper, fenugreek seeds and garlic.

REGIONAL CLASSIC **künefe** a dessert made with fine strands of pastry dough called *tel kadayıf.* Fresh cheese is placed between two layers of butter-soaked pastry. After baking, it is drenched in syrup and served piping hot.

NATIONAL FAVORITE **lahmacun** a popular, pizza-like street food made of soft, thin dough thinly spread with a spicy paste of minced lamb, tomatoes, green peppers, garlic, onion and hot red pepper. Traditionally, lamb's tail fat was used to hold the paste together. The bread has characteristic rows of imprints made by the bakers with their fingers.

lâhana kapama a boiled cabbage head stuffed with meat.

lâkerda salted bonito.

lâpa a mushy rice stew.

REGIONAL CLASSIC **Lâz böreği** a dessert made with thin layers of pastry dough called *yufka* filled with rice pudding, subtly flavored with black pepper; a specialty of the Black Sea region of Turkey.

levrek balığı o graten baked sea bass with grated cheese.

levrek fırında baked sea bass.

levrek ızgara grilled sea bass.

levrek pilâki a cold casserole of sea bass with vegetables cooked in olive oil.

limon tatlısı deep-fried, lemon-flavored pastries soaked in syrup.

lokma balls of fried, sweet dough soaked in syrup; a specialty of   RICH
İzmir, a city in the central Aegean region of Turkey.

lor tatlısı syrup-soaked pastries containing a soft goat's cheese called *lor*.

lüfer buğulama poached *lüfer*, a fish similar to the bluefish.

mahallebi see *muhallebi*.

mançı an appetizer of eggplant and yogurt.

mangalda et meat cooked on a brazier. Many roadside eating places advertise this dish with the colloquialism, *et mangal*, printed on large, hand written signs.

mantar çorbası mushroom soup.

mantar sote sautéed mushrooms.

mantarlı börek mushroom *börek*.   FLAVORFUL

mantarlı ördek duck with mushrooms.

mantı small cheese- or minced meat-filled pastas, which are   NATIONAL FAVORITE
boiled and sometimes also baked, and served smothered in a yogurt and garlic sauce flavored with mint, or a tomato sauce. They have two distinct forms. One version is made by placing pieces of filling in neat rows on top of a rolled circle of dough and then completely covering it with another circle of dough. Individual, pillow-shaped squares of pasta are formed by cutting between the rows of fillings, usually with a tool to make serrated edges. This type of *mantı* is common in İstanbul. A more labor-intensive product is made by cutting rows of small squares from one circle of dough, topping each with a bit of filling and then bringing up the four corners of a square and pinching their tips together above the filling. This preparation is typical of central Anatolia. Also see *tatar böreği*.

mantı böreği a *börek* filled with minced meat, onions, red pepper, parsley and mint. The preparation is rolled like a jelly roll and then coiled. Individual rolls are topped with a yogurt sauce sprinkled with red pepper flakes.

marul salatası a salad with romaine lettuce, scallions and mint.

maydanozlu yumurta beaten eggs with parsley.

mayonezli kırlangıç gurnard fish with a mayonnaise sauce.

menecit kahvesi coffee made from wild pistachios.

menekşe şerbeti sherbet made from violet-petal extract.

menekşe şurubu syrup made from violet-petal extract.

WONDERFUL   **menemen** a lightly cooked omelette of beaten eggs, tomatoes and green peppers.

Mengen çorbası soup with milk, yogurt, rice and bits of tomato and potato; a specialty of the city of Mengen in north-central Anatolia.

mercimek çorbası lentil soup.

REGIONAL CLASSIC   **mercimek köftesi** a cold appetizer made of mashed lentils and bulgur formed into small oval patties.

mercimekli bükme böreği a *börek* filled with a green lentil mixture.

Mevlânâ a pizza-like preparation made with oval-shaped *pide* bread covered with a mixture of chopped lamb and *tulum* cheese, topped with melted butter. A specialty of the central Anatolian city of Konya, this dish is named after the thirteenth century mystic, Mevlânâ, as is an appetizer made with humus and *kaşar* cheese.

Mevlevî pilâvı rice pilaf with lamb, chestnuts, carrots and chickpeas, a dish associated with the whirling dervishes, followers of the thirteenth century mystic Mevlânâ.

meyhane pilâvı bulgur pilaf with minced meat, green peppers and tomatoes.

mezgit tavası fried whiting.

mıhlama a fried mixture of eggs, minced lamb, tomatoes, spinach and *pastırma.*

mısır ekmeği corn bread.

REGIONAL CLASSIC   **mısır unlu hamsi tava** anchovy-like fish called *hamsi* breaded with corn flour and fried.

midye çorbası mussel soup.

midye dolması a cold appetizer of mussels stuffed in the shell with a mixture of rice, pine nuts and currants.

midye pilâkisi mussels, potatoes, carrots, tomatoes and garlic cloves, sautéed in olive oil, then served chilled as an appetizer.

REGIONAL CLASSIC   **midye tavası** an appetizer of deep-fried mussels on wooden skewers. It traditionally is served with *tarator,* a ground nut sauce.

midyeli pilâv pilaf with mussels.

morina ızgarası broiled cod fillet.

morina tavası fried cod fillet.

NATIONAL FAVORITE   **muhallebi** milk pudding; also spelled *mahallebi.*

muhallebili baklava baklava filled with a creamy semolina mixture.

muhammara an appetizer consisting of a paste made of ground REGIONAL CLASSIC
walnuts, roasted red peppers, bread crumbs, hot red peppers
and garlic, mixed with olive oil and seasoned with pomegranate
syrup and lemon juice.

musakka a casserole of sliced vegetables, especially eggplant,
topped with a seasoned minced meat mixture.

muska böreği small triangle-shaped *böreks* made with thin DELICIOUS
sheets of pastry dough called *yufka,* which contain a meat or
cheese mixture.

müceddere a pilaf of lentils and bulgur with olive oil.

mücver fritters made with grated squash or zucchini, white NATIONAL FAVORITE
cheese and onions, and flavored with dill.

naneli oğmaç çorbası a mint-flavored soup with yogurt and small
round beads of homemade pasta.

nar ekşili patlıcanlı köfte grilled, minced lamb balls cooked with
roasted eggplant and flavored with a sauce of tomato and
pomegranate syrup.

nar şerbeti a lemonade-like drink made with pomegranates.

nar şurubuyla yoğurt a dessert with pomegranate sauce and
sweetened yogurt cream, made by adding sugar to yogurt after
it is strained to remove the water.

narlı çorba pomegranate soup.

nevzine a dessert made with sesame paste and topped with
pekmez, a molasses-like syrup made by boiling grape juice until
it is reduced.

nohut çorbası a cream-based soup of puréed chickpeas and INTERESTING
celery root, flavored with red pepper.

nohut ezmesi a spread made with mashed chickpeas.

nohut salatası chickpea salad.

nohutlu işkembe lamb tripe with chickpeas in a garlic and
vinegar sauce.

nohutlu kuzu paçası lamb's trotters with chickpeas.

nohutlu mantı pasta stuffed with chickpeas.

nohutlu patlıcan dolması eggplant stuffed with chickpeas.

nokul rolls filled with sesame and walnut paste, flavored with TASTY
cinnamon, cloves and rose-petal extract.

ordövr tabağı a plate of several different appetizers.

orman kebabı lamb with carrots, tomatoes and potatoes.

oruk oblong, tapered balls of bulgur, poked with a finger to make an opening, and filled with a mixture of minced lamb, walnuts, flat-leaf parsley, onions and cumin.

oturtma a casserole of eggplant and cubed lamb. It also is the name for the method of deep-frying hollowed-out vegetables and then cooking them with a minced meat stuffing.

öcce a fritter made with eggs, flour, onion, garlic and mint.

ördek dolması stuffed roast duck.

örgülü pilâv rice pilaf with diced chicken, covered with a pastry lattice. It is made like a pie with a lattice pastry shell and inverted before serving.

Özbek pilâvı rice pilaf containing lamb, carrots and onions; a dish attributed to the Uzbek people of central Asia.

paça a soup made with sheep's or goat's trotters.

palamut tava fried bonito.

pancar dolması stuffed beets.

pancar salatası beet salad.

pancar turşusu pickled beet salad.

papaz yahnisi a ragout with veal, onions and garlic in a sauce flavored with allspice, cinnamon and red pepper.

parmak patates strips of fried potatoes resembling thick French fries.

pastırmalı yumurta eggs fried with *pastırma,* the dried and salted meat preparation cured with a paste of red pepper, fenugreek seeds and garlic.

patates ezmesi çorbası cream of potato soup.

patates köftesi balls of mashed potatoes and grated *kaşar* cheese, dipped in flour, beaten egg and bread crumbs and deep-fried.

patates oturtması a stew of potatoes, tomatoes and peppers.

patates salatası potato salad.

patatesli börek a *börek* filled with a potato and onion mixture.

patatesli buğu pirzolası steamed chops with potatoes.

patatesli güveç potato casserole.

patatesli omlet potato omelette.

patlıcan kızartması fried eggplant.

patlıcan oturtma a dish of thick eggplant slices spread with minced lamb, and topped with tomato and green bell pepper.

patlıcan salatası a warm or cold salad made with mashed, roasted eggplant in olive oil, lemon juice and vinegar. It is less commonly the name of a cold salad made with thinly sliced eggplant, green pepper strips and quartered tomatoes, which are fried in olive oil and dressed with wine and vinegar. **FABULOUS**

patlıcan turşusu eggplant pickles.

patlıcan ve biber salatası a cold salad of roasted eggplant and hot peppers, simmered in olive oil, garlic and red pepper, and flavored with a touch of vinegar.

patlıcanlı bıldırcın quail with baked eggplant.

patlıcanlı börek a *börek* with eggplant filling.

patlıcanlı kebap lamb and eggplant casserole.

patlıcanlı köfte Gaziantep usülü eggplant stuffed with flattened, sausage-shaped pieces of minced lamb, covered with a sauce of roasted peppers and tomatoes, and simmered. This preparation is a specialty of Gaziantep, a city in southeastern Turkey.

patlıcanlı makarna eggplant with macaroni.

patlıcanlı pide *pide* bread filled with an eggplant mixture.

pazı salatası chard salad.

pekmez helvası halvah made with *pekmez,* a concentrated syrup made by boiling grape juice.

pekmezli ayva dolması quince stuffed with a mixture of minced lamb, rice and *pekmez,* a concentrated syrup made by boiling grape juice. **REGIONAL CLASSIC**

perdeli pilâv rice pilaf with diced chicken, pine nuts and almonds, encased in pastry.

peynirli irmik helvası halvah made with semolina and cheese.

peynirli kabak zucchini halves filled with a cheese mixture.

peynirli pırasa fritters made with chopped leeks and cheese.

peynirli pide *pide* bread spread with a cheese topping and baked. **NATIONAL FAVORITE**

peynirli poğaça a turnover filled with a cheese mixture.

peynirli tost a grilled cheese sandwich; also called *tost.*

peynirli yumurtalı patlıcan eggplant with cheese and egg.

piliç çevirme chicken roasted on a spit.

piliç kâğıtta young (spring) chicken baked in parchment paper.

piliç kuşhane kebabı small pieces of sautéed chicken.

piliçli bamya okra with chicken.

pirinçli piliç chicken with rice.

piruhi a type of cheese-filled *börek.*

pirzolalı kâğıt kebabı lamb chops baked in parchment.

REGIONAL CLASSIC **piyaz** a cold bean salad in vinaigrette.

poğaça a flaky cheese pastry.

portakal peltesi orange pudding.

portakal salatası a salad of orange slices topped with pieces of black olives and thin slices of red onions, drizzled with olive oil.

portakal salçası orange sauce.

portakallı bisküvi orange-flavored cookie or biscuit.

NATIONAL FAVORITE **puf böreği** a cheese- or meat-filled turnover of puff pastry, which swells when fried.

revani a syrup-soaked cake made with semolina, which usually is inverted after baking.

HEAVENLY **saç arası** a syrup-soaked dessert made of thin sheets of pastry dough called *yufka,* topped with pistachios. A few sheets of dough are gently pushed together to form a narrow strip, which is then coiled and flattened to make a disk. It is fried on a convex griddle called a *saç* before the syrup and nuts are added.

EXCELLENT CHOICE **saç böreği** a *börek* filled with meat, potatoes or cheese. It is covered with butter and fried on a convex griddle called a *saç.*

saç kavurma see *kavurma.*

saç kebap long, thin strips of lamb cooked with onions and tomatoes.

saçaklı mantı toasted noodles with shredded chicken, topped with yogurt and garlic sauce.

sade pilâv plain rice.

safranlı pilâv rice pilaf flavored with saffron.

sahan köftesi meatball stew cooked in a shallow baking pan.

sahanda sucuk fried, spicy sausage.

NATIONAL FAVORITE **sahleb** a hot, sweetened milk drink flavored and thickened with *sahleb,* or powdered orchid root, and sprinkled with cinnamon.

sakızlı dondurma ice cream flavored with *sakız,* the resin from an acacia evergreen tree.

sakızlı muhallebi milk pudding flavored with *sakız,* the resin from an acacia evergreen tree.

saksı kebabı a dish of diced lamb, potatoes and tomatoes, piled on top of half an eggplant.

salçalı uskumru mackerel in tomato sauce.

salma a stew with rice.

samsa tatlısı a syrup-soaked flaky pastry filled with a paste of ground walnuts, hazelnuts, almonds and semolina.

saray çorbası a creamy soup with mushrooms and wine.

sarığı burma a nut-filled dessert made with layers of thin pastry dough called *yufka,* rolled up like a jelly roll on a thin rolling pin, or *oklava.* The pastry roll is then slightly puckered by gently pushing it from both ends towards the center before it is removed from the rolling pin. Several of these rolls are placed end-to-end in a round, shallow baking pan, forming a coil. **SCRUMPTIOUS**

sarımsaklı karides shrimp with garlic.

sarımsaklı köfte balls of bulgur in a garlic sauce. **REGIONAL CLASSIC**

sarımsaklı patlıcan eggplant with garlic.

sarımsaklı sirkeli salça a garlic and vinegar sauce.

sarma kadayıfı a dessert made with thin strands of pastry dough called *tel kadayıf,* or simply *kadayıf,* filled with pistachios. Several lengths of this dessert are placed end-to-end in a round baking pan to form a coil.

sebze çorbası vegetable soup.

sebzeli incik kebabı lamb shanks with vegetables.

sebzeli piliç budu güveci a vegetable casserole with chicken thighs.

semirsek a *börek* filled with lamb, onions, egg yolk and parsley.

semizotu piyazı a salad with purslane. **REGIONAL CLASSIC**

sığır dili ox tongue.

sigara böreği a *börek* with a cheese or meat filling, rolled into small cylinders resembling cigarettes, and deep fried or baked. **NATIONAL FAVORITE**

simit kebap a kebab made with bulgur.

sini köftesi a baked, layered dish made with minced lamb. Two layers of a lamb and bulgur mixture are separated by a mixture of lamb, walnuts and pistachios. The ingredients for this dish are the same as those for *içli köfte,* but the preparation is much simpler. **REGIONAL CLASSIC**

sirkeli patlıcan eggplant simmered in a tomato, garlic and vinegar sauce.

sirkeli sarımsaklı biber ızgara a cold appetizer of roasted red peppers sprinkled with a sauce of garlic and vinegar.

sirkeli sarımsaklı pancar salatası a salad of beets marinated with garlic and vinegar.

sivediz a preparation of lamb, yogurt, chickpeas, garlic cloves and scallions.

soğan çorbası onion soup.

soğan piyazı a cold onion relish.

soğanlı patatesli mıhlama a fried mixture of eggs with onions and potatoes.

soğanlı yahni a ragout of diced beef cooked with tomatoes and onions, flavored with vinegar and allspice.

soğanlı yumurta cooked eggs in a bed of fried onions, flavored with allspice and cinnamon.

soğuk domates çorbası cold tomato soup.

som fırında baked salmon.

söyürme eggplant purée.

su böreği a labor-intensive dish made with circles of rolled pastry dough, somewhat thicker than those for a *börek,* which are individually boiled, stacked in alternating layers with a meat or white cheese filling, and baked.

su muhallebisi a pudding flavored with rose water.

sucuklu köfte balls made of *sucuk,* a spicy sausage mixture.

sucuklu pide *pide* bread topped with the spicy sausage called *sucuk.*

sucuklu tost a toasted sandwich made with the spicy sausage called *sucuk.*

sucuklu yumurta eggs with a spicy sausage called *sucuk.*

Sultan Reşad pilâvı buttered pilaf with eggplant, tomatoes and tiny meatballs, a preparation presumably associated with Sultan Reşad, who reigned from 1909 to 1918.

sultan sarma pounded tenderloin fillet wrapped around a mixture of sautéed mushrooms and onions, pistachio nuts and *kaşar* cheese, and grilled.

sünger tatlısı small sponge cakes of semolina and rice flour, soaked in syrup and coated with ground nuts.

süt kuzusu kâğıt kebabı pieces of suckling lamb baked in parchment paper.

sütlâç rice pudding.

sütlü pirinç çorbası a milk-based rice soup.

sütlü tel kadayıf a dessert made with thin threads of pastry dough called *tel kadayıf* stuffed with a nut and thick cream filling, in a milk sauce.

süzme yoğurt an appetizer of yogurt that has been thickened by straining it through cloth to remove the water.

şafak çorbası a milk-based tomato soup thickened with flour.

şalgam a drink of beet and carrot juice flavored with lemon, which often is drunk with *rakı,* Turkey's national liquor distilled from grapes. Some believe the effect of the alcohol is conteracted by drinking *şalgam* at the same time.

şalgam mussakka a casserole of turnip roots and minced lamb.

şalgam suyu beet juice.

şambaba tatlısı a dessert made with alternating layers of a semolina, milk and sugar mixture and crushed nuts. When baked, it is soaked in syrup and cut into pieces.

şaraplı dana fried veal steak simmered in a white wine sauce.

şaraplı sazan balığı carp in wine.

şaşlık lamb marinated in olive oil, salt and paprika and grilled. It is garnished with sautéed mushrooms and pearl onions.

şauşuka an appetizer of chopped eggplant, tomato, onion and garlic.

şehriyeli pilâv a pilaf made with vermicelli.

şehriyeli tavuk suyu chicken broth with vermicelli.

şekerli ayva dolması quince stuffed with a minced meat and rice mixture, flavored with allspice and cinnamon.

şekerpare balls of sweet dough baked like cookies, topped with an almond and soaked in sugar syrup.

Şirvan pilâvı rice with meat and carrots, a dish attributed to a region in northeast Iran.

şiş kebabı lamb marinated in milk and olive oil, and grilled on a skewer.

şiş kebabı Güneydoğu Anadolu usülü spicy lamb shish kebabs marinated in hot red pepper and herbs in the style of the southeastern region of Turkey.

şiş köfte sausage-shaped pieces of minced lamb grilled on a skewer.

tahinli katmer flaky pastry filled with sesame paste.

talaş böreği a *börek* filled with pistachios and thin strips of lamb.

talaş kebabı puff pastry, typically square, filled with a minced meat mixture.

tandır kebabı a dish of roast lamb and onions baked in a clay-lined oven called a *tandır.*

tarama a salad of fish roe in olive oil and lemon juice.

tarator salatası a sauce of pulverized walnuts, garlic and chopped parsley, in sesame oil and lemon juice.

taratorlu karnıbahar a cold appetizer of cooked cauliflower, served with a nut sauce.

tarçınlı pilâv cinnamon-flavored rice pilaf with raisins and pine nuts.

NATIONAL FAVORITE **tarhana çorbası** a soup made with *tarhana,* and sometimes minced lamb. *Tarhana* is a dough preparation containing yogurt and pulverized tomatoes, red peppers and onions, which is allowed to ferment. It is then air dried, crumbled and stored at room temperature as a soup base.

NATIONAL FAVORITE **tas kebabı** braised lamb with tomatoes, potatoes and onions, and flavored with allspice or thyme. The mixture is placed in a bowl, which is then overturned in the center of a mound of rice.

taş kadayıf see *yassı kakayıf.*

Tatar böreği boiled, meat-filled squares of pastry dough topped with a yogurt sauce and drizzled with melted butter and red pepper; a dish attributed to the Tatars. It is similar to the preparation called *mantı;* see *mantı.*

tatlı yoğurt sweet yogurt cream. Yogurt is thickened to a cream by straining excess liquid through a cloth or strainer. The yogurt is then sweetened.

tavada köfte breaded and fried meatballs.

tavşan kebabı rabbit kebab.

tavuk böreği a *börek* with chicken filling.

tavuk çorbası cream of chicken soup.

NATIONAL FAVORITE **tavuk göğsü** a rice flour pudding containing very finely shredded chicken breast. A mixture of the same ingredients is also used to make a variation of the dessert called *kazan dibi.*

tavuk göğsü kazan dibi see *kazan dibi.*

tavuk köftesi meatballs made with a minced chicken mixture.

tavuk suyuyla şehriye çorbası chicken soup with vermicelli.

NATIONAL FAVORITE **tavuk yahnisi** a chicken stew.

tavuklu beğendi chicken with eggplant purée.

tavuklu güveç chicken and vegetable casserole.

tavuklu makarna a casserole of macaroni layered with strips of chicken in a cream sauce.

taze bakla çorbası fava bean soup served with yogurt and dill sauce.

taze baklalı dereotulu pilâv pilaf with fresh fava beans and dill.

teke balığı suflesi shrimp soufflé.

IRRESISTIBLE **tel kadayıf** a dessert made with layers of thin pastry dough strands resembling shredded wheat, which are baked and then soaked in syrup. Fillings can include ground nuts and *kaymak,* a rich, thick cream firm enough to be sliced.

tencere külbastı lamb cutlets in tomato sauce, cooked in a kettle, or *tencere*.

tepsi kebabı a mixture of ground lamb, onion, hot pepper and flat-leaf parsley, baked in a shallow tray.

terbiyeli köfte meatballs in an egg yolk and lemon sauce.   NATIONAL FAVORITE

terbiyeli paça sheep trotters soup thickened and flavored with an egg yolk and lemon sauce.

terbiyeli pırasa leeks in an egg yolk and lemon sauce.

terbiyeli tavuk suyu chicken broth with an egg yolk and lemon sauce.

tereyağlı kaymak an omelette prepared with eggs, cream, corn flour and butter.

tereyağlı kereviz celery root sautéed in butter.

tez pişti a baked rice pudding.

tost see *peynirli tost*.

Trabzon kızartması an appetizer of deep-fried eggplant in a   REGIONAL CLASSIC
garlic and yogurt sauce; a specialty of Trabzon, a city on the eastern Black Sea coast.

tulumba tatlısı fried, cylindrical pastry with a fluted surface,   SWEET
soaked in syrup and sprinkled with ground almonds.

turşu biber pickled pepper.

turşu suyu pickle juice, enjoyed for its refreshing quality.

tutmaç aşı see *kesme çorbası*.

tutmaç çorbası a soup with yogurt, homemade noodles and small meatballs.

tuzda balık fish baked in salt.

tuzlu kurabiye salty cracker.

tuzlu yoğurt an appetizer of salty yogurt with bits of red pepper.

Türk pilâvı carrot pilaf.

türlü a hearty, mixed vegetable and meat casserole; also called *türlü güveç*.

türlü güveç see *türlü*.

ufak köfte a dish of lamb, chickpeas and two different-sized balls   REGIONAL CLASSIC
of minced meat and bulgur, in a yogurt sauce. The larger balls are stuffed; they have been poked with a finger to make a hole, and filled with a mixture of minced meat and nuts. A similar version of this dish with a tart, tomato sauce rather than yogurt is called *ekşili ufak köfte*.

un çorbası a white soup prepared with flour, butter, milk and broth.

un helvası flour halvah.

un kurabiyesi flour cookie.

Urfa kebabı long, sausage-shaped pieces of minced lamb, grilled on a skewer and served on top of toasted pieces of *pide* bread that have been softened with broth; a specialty of the city of Şanlıurfa, formerly Urfa, a city in southeastern Anatolia.

REGIONAL CLASSIC **uskumru dolması** a cold appetizer of stuffed mackerel. The flesh, bones and entrails of an uncleaned fish are most carefully removed through the mouth or gills, leaving the skin and head intact. The extracted flesh is mixed with pine nuts, currants, crushed walnuts, finely chopped herbs and various spices and stuffed back into the skin, restoring the original shape. The fish is then breaded and fried in olive oil.

uskumru kâğıtta mackerel baked in parchment paper.

uskumru pilâkisi a cold dish of mackerel cooked in olive oil.

uskumru taratorlu an appetizer of poached mackerel served with a sauce of ground hazelnuts, minced garlic and vinegar.

üzüm hoşafı raisin compote.

vanilyalı kurabiye vanilla cookie.

vezir parmağı fried finger-shaped pastries soaked in syrup.

vişne hoşafı sour cherry compote.

vişne tiridi sour cherry pudding.

vişneli ekmek sour cherry bread.

yağlı ekmek deep-fried slices of egg-coated bread, similar in taste to our French toast.

NATIONAL FAVORITE **yalancı dolma** meatless stuffed grape leaves, which typically contain rice, pine nuts and currants. *Yalancı* means liar and refers to the fact that such meatless *dolmas* are imitations of the meat-filled ones. See *yaprak dolması*.

NATIONAL FAVORITE **yaprak dolması** grape leaves stuffed with rice, pine nuts and currants; meat may also be added. When this dish lacks meat, it often is called *yalancı dolma;* see *yalancı dolma.*

yassı kadayıf a syrup-soaked dessert made with a flat, crumpet-like pancake, which is soaked in milk, coated in beaten egg and flour, and deep-fried. Also called *taş kadayıf* and *Arap kadayıfı.*

yayık ayranı churned *ayran*, a lightly salted drink of yogurt and water.

yayla çorbası mint-flavored soup with yogurt and rice; also called
yoğurt çorbası.

yaz meyveleri kompostosu a compote of summer fruit.

yaz türlüsü a summer vegetable and meat dish.

yaz yumurtası eggs fried in depressions made in a mixture of sautéed onion, tomato and pepper.

yelpaze fan-shaped cookie.

yeşil biberli kılıç a cold dish of swordfish steaks cooked with green peppers.

yeşil biberli salça green pepper sauce.

yeşil fıstıklı krema milk pudding with chopped pistachio nuts.

yeşil mercimek çorbası cream of green lentil soup.

yeşil pilâv pilaf with parsley and dill.

yeşil soğanlı et braised lamb with scallions.

yoğurt çorbası see *yayla çorbası.*

yoğurt salçası yogurt sauce. It has garlic when used with meats and fried vegetables; sugar, when used with fresh fruit.

yoğurt tatlısı a cake made with yogurt. The cake is cut into squares or diamonds, which are then soaked in syrup.

yoğurtlu havuç salatası a salad of grated carrots in yogurt sauce.

yoğurtlu kabak a cold dish of sautéed, grated zucchini mixed with yogurt and garlic.

yoğurtlu kebap pieces of grilled, marinated lamb placed on top of
torn pieces of *pide* bread, and topped with both a garlic yogurt sauce and a roasted tomato sauce.

yoğurtlu makarna macaroni in yogurt sauce.

yoğurtlu pancar salatası beet salad with yogurt.

yoğurtlu patlıcan biber ızgara a cold appetizer of roasted eggplant and peppers covered with a yogurt and garlic sauce.

yoğurtlu semizotu a casserole of purslane and ground lamb served with yogurt sauce.

yoğurtlu yeşil fıstıklı kek a cake made with yogurt and finely ground pistachios.

yufka içinde tavuk sheets of thin dough called *yufka* wrapped
around a chicken mixture.

yufkalı pilâv a pie made with thin sheets of pastry dough called *yufka,* filled with a rice and chicken mixture.

yulaf ezmesi oatmeal porridge.

yumurta dolması deviled eggs.

yumurtalı kabak kalye squash served with eggs.

REGIONAL CLASSIC   yuvarlama a dish of small meat and bulgur balls in a spicy tomato sauce, which is similar to the preparation called *ekşili ufak köfte*. It also includes dough balls made of flour and water that are slightly larger than chickpeas, and is given a piquant taste by the addition of unripe plum paste.

NATIONAL FAVORITE   yüksük çorbası a soup with chickpeas, tiny meatballs and small round noodles traditionally cut out with a thimble.

NATIONAL FAVORITE   zerde a saffron-flavored pudding made with rice. The surface is decorated with pistachios, pine nuts, hazelnuts, currants and pomegranate seeds.

zeytinli ekmek bread made with olive oil and black olives.

zeytinyağlı bakla ezmesi a cold dish of mashed fava beans cooked in olive oil and covered with a lemon and dill sauce.

zeytinyağlı biber dolması a cold dish of stuffed peppers cooked in olive oil.

zeytinyağlı dolma içi a mixture of rice, pine nuts and currants, flavored with dill, mint, allspice and cinnamon and cooked in olive oil. It is a stuffing for various vegetables.

zeytinyağlı domates dolması a cold dish of stuffed tomatoes cooked in olive oil.

zeytinyağlı enginar a cold dish of artichoke hearts cooked in olive oil and garnished with dill.

zeytinyağlı enginar dolması a cold dish of artichokes stuffed with a rice and pistachio mixture and cooked in olive oil.

zeytinyağlı fasulye a cold dish of white beans cooked with garlic cloves and olive oil.

zeytinyağlı kereviz a cold dish of celery root cooked in olive oil.

zeytinyağlı lâhana sarması a cold dish of cabbage leaves wrapped around a filling and cooked with olive oil.

NATIONAL FAVORITE   zeytinyağlı patlıcan dolması a cold appetizer of stuffed cabbage leaves cooked in oil.

zeytinyağlı pırasa a cold dish of leeks cooked in olive oil.

NATIONAL FAVORITE   zeytinyağlı yaprak dolması a cold dish of grape leaves stuffed with a mixture of rice, pine nuts and currants, and cooked in olive oil.

zeytinyağlı yeşil fasulye a cold dish of green beans cooked in olive oil.

zırbaç sheep's trotters stewed with saffron and garlic.

Foods & Flavors Guide

This chapter is a comprehensive list of foods, spices, kitchen utensils and cooking terminology in Turkish, with English translations. The list will be helpful in interpreting menus since it is impossible to cover all the flavors or combinations possible for certain dishes. It will also be useful for shopping in both supermarkets and the lively and fascinating outdoor markets.

abur cubur junk food.

acı bitter; means hot, if describing peppers.

acı badem bitter almond.

acılı with hot pepper.

acur a long, thin variety of cucumber.

açma a type of turnover.

ada çayı sage; also called *meryemiye*. *Ada çayı* is also sage tea, taken as a cure for bronchitis. Another name for this herbal tea is *dağ çayı*, or mountain tea.

ağaç çileği raspberry; also called *ahududu.*

ağaç kavunu citron.

ahçı tabağı a sampling of everything the chef has made on a given day.

ahlat wild pear.

ahtapot octopus.

ahududu raspberry; also called *ağaç çileği.*

aile gazinosu an establishment combining dining and family entertainment in a setting where alcohol is not served, in contrast to *gazino,* a similar establishment where alcohol is served.

aile salonu (family hall) that part of a restaurant set aside for family dining (i.e., single men are not welcome). A similar expression, *aileye mahsustur,* means reserved for families.

aileye mahsustur see *aile salonu.*

ak ekmek white bread.

akasya balı acacia honey.

akciğer lung.

akşam yemeği dinner.

alabalık trout.

alabaş red cabbage.

alakok yumurta soft-boiled egg.

alkollü içki alcohol. Especially during Ramadan, alcoholic drinks may be hard to get. Note that *ispirto* is rubbing alcohol; it is not meant for drinks.

altın gold or golden.

altın kefal golden mullet.

altıntop grapefruit; also called *greyfrut.*

amarak sweet marjoram; also called *şile* or *mercanköşk.*

Amerikan fıstığı peanut; also called *yerfıstığı.*

ananas pineapple.

anason anise or aniseed.

ançuez anchovy.

ançuez ezmesi anchovy paste.

Antep fıstığı pistachio; also called *şamfıstığı.*

Antep peyniri a ripe cheese made in Antep (now Gaziantep), a city in southeastern Anatolia. The cheese is aged for several months in an earthenware pot.

aperitif apéritif or appetizer.

ara sıcağı a hot course between the appetizer (*meze*) and main courses.

Arap (Arabic) darısı buckwheat.

Arap (Arabic) kadayıfı crumpet-like pancake; also called *yassı kadayıf.*

ardıç juniper.

ardıç tohumu juniper seeds.

armut pear.

Arnavut (Albanian) biberi cayenne pepper.

arpa barley.

arpacık soğanı shallot.

asma grapevine or vine.

asma yaprağı grapevine leaf; often simply called *yaprak*, or leaf, and implying a grapevine leaf.

aspur safflower, a thistle-like herb. Be cautioned that it is sometimes falsely marketed as more expensive saffron. Safflower is used as a seasoning in the southeastern region of Turkey (see *aspurlu pilav* in *Menu Guide*). Also spelled *haspir* and *hespir.*

aş cooked food.

aşçı cook.

aşçıbaşı chef.

aşçılık cuisine or cookery.

aşık knuckle bone.

aşurelik buğday hulled whole wheat, a key component in the pudding called *aşure* (see *Menu Guide*). Also called *dövme*.

av eti game.

ayçiçeği sunflower.

ayran a popular and refreshing drink made of yogurt beaten with an equal amount of water and lightly salted. A few ice cubes usually are added to the glass.

ayva quince.

az pişmiş underdone (rare).

az şekerli slightly sweetened with sugar.

bacak leg.

badem almond.

badem ezmesi almond paste or marzipan.

badem kurabiyesi macaroon.

badem yağı almond oil.

badi duck; also called *ördek*.

Bafra pirinci a type of rice from Cyprus.

bağırsak intestine; also means sausage casing.

bahar spice; also means the season Spring. Note that the plural of spice is *baharat*.

baharatçı spice seller.

bahçe garden.

bahşiş tip.

bakanak trotter; also called *paça*.

bakkal grocer.

bakla broadbean, fava bean or horse bean. These beans are not eaten whole unless the pods are very immature.

baklava any of several delicious syrup-soaked confections made with layers of thin pastry dough called *yufka*, ground nuts and sometimes a thick cream called *kaymak*.

baklavacı maker of *baklava*.

bakliyat dried bean or legume.

bal honey.

bal kabağı pumpkin; also called *kabak*.

balık fish.

balık yumurtası fish roe, usually from mullet, which are salted, sun-dried and encased in wax to keep the still-oily roe fresh. The waxed roe are eaten thinly sliced and sprinkled with freshly squeezed lemon juice.

balıklar the plural of fish. On menus, this word is found at the head of the fish section.

ballı honeyed.

bamya okra.

bandırma a type of confection made with walnuts; see *sucuk*.

barbunya large (older) specimen of red mullet. Young specimens are called *tekir*. It is also the name of a small, red bean.

bardak drinking glass.

basılıkum sweet basil; also called *fesleğen*.

baş head.

batonsale a thin, salted bread stick; compare with *krikrak*.

bayat stale.

bazlama flat, usually unleavened bread, about 1 inch thick and 6 to 8 inches in diameter, which is baked on a griddle.

Bektaşi üzümü gooseberry.

bergamot a lemon-like citrus fruit, whose grated rind is used to flavor tea and some sweetmeats.

berlam hake.

beyaz white.

beyaz peynir the common, lightly salted cheese made from sheep's milk. It is stored in brine and rinsed with water before eating.

beyaz şarap white wine.

beyaz turp white radish.

beyin brain.

beykin bacon.

bezelye pea.

bıçak knife.

bıldırcın quail.

biber pepper.

biber tanesi peppercorn; also called *dövülmemiş biber*.

biberiye rosemary.

biberli peppery.

biberlik pepper shaker.

biftek beefsteak.

bir buçuk porsiyon one and one-half times a single helping of food. Kebab houses, for example, often provide a choice in serving size.

bir porsiyon a single helping of food.

bira beer.

birahane beer pub or brewery.

bisküvi biscuit, cracker or cookie, which can be sweet or salty.

bonfile fillet of beef.

bostan vegetable garden.

bostan patlıcanı the large, round variety of eggplant.

boy otu fenugreek; also called *çemenotu.*

boza a thick winter drink made with fermented millet. Cinnamon and *leblebi*, or roasted chickpeas, traditionally are sprinkled on top.

böbrek kidney.

böğürtlen blackberry.

börek a savory meat- or cheese-filled flaky pastry made with thinly rolled sheets of dough called *yufka.* They are available in a variety of shapes.

börekçi shop serving *börek.*

börekler the plural of *börek.* On menus, this words heads the *börek* section.

börülce kidney bean or black-eyed bean.

Brezilya kestanesi Brazil nut.

Brüksel lâhanası Brussels sprout.

buğday wheat.

buğulama steamed.

bulama molasses-like syrup; see *pekmez.*

bulamaç a paste or thick soup.

bulgur hulled whole wheat that has been partially cooked with steam, then dried and coarsely ground. A more-finely ground bulgur, called *simit, düğü* or *ince bulgur*, is a key component of several minced meat mixtures for dishes such as *çiğ köfte* and *ufak köfte* (see this *Guide* and the *Menu Guide*). Note that cracked wheat, which is also coarsely ground, hulled whole wheat, differs from bulgur in that it is not partially cooked by steam before being ground, and therefore takes longer to cook.

bumbar large intestine; also sausage or sausage casing.

but thigh.

buz ice.

buz gibi ice cold.

buzağı calf; also called *dana.*

buzlu çay iced tea.

buzlu su ice water.

büfe a small shop or booth selling snacks and beverages.

bütün domates konservesi canned whole tomatoes.

büyük large.

FOODS & FLAVORS GUIDE

can eriği (soul or life plum) a tart, unripe green plum.

cere otu coriander seed; also called *kişniş*.

ceviz walnut.

cezve a long-handled, wide-necked pot used to brew Turkish coffee. It is available in several sizes.

ciğer liver; also called *karaciğer*.

cin gin.

çağanoz crab; also called *yengeç*.

çağla bademi a green or unripe almond.

çakal eriği wild plum.

çalı shrub or bush.

çalı fasulyesi bush bean or string bean.

çam balı dark, pine-scented honey.

çam fıstığı pine nut.

çamuka smelt; also called *gümüş balığı*.

çapak fresh-water bream.

çarliston biberi a long, yellowish-green pepper somewhat larger than the dark-green variety called *sivri biber*.

çarşı a large, permanent, indoor market; compare with *pazar*.

çatal fork.

çavdar rye.

çavdar ekmeği this is the name for both rye and pumpernickel bread.

çavdar unu rye flour.

çay tea.

çay bahçesi tea garden.

çay demliği teapot.

çay kaşığı teaspoon.

çaydanlık tea kettle.

çebiç young goat.

çekirdek seed; also called *tohum*. Pumpkin seeds, or *kabak çekirdeği*, a popular street snack, are commonly referred to simply as *çekirdek*.

çekirdeksiz kuru üzüm seedless raisin.

çekirdeksiz üzüm seedless grape; also called *sultani*.

çeltik unhusked rice.

çemen a paste made primarily of red pepper, fenugreek seeds and garlic, which is used as a coating and flavoring for the dried meat preparation called *pastırma*. It also flavors certain dishes such as *külbastı* (see *Menu Guide*).

çemenotu fenugreek; also called *boy otu*.

çerez see *meze*.

Çerkes (Circassian) refers to the Circassian region of Russia from which the classic appetizer called *Çerkes tavuğu*, or Circassian chicken, derives (see *Menu Guide*).

çeşitleri a selection of . . .

çeşitli various, assorted or mixed; another word for this is *karışık*.

çevirme meat roasted on a spit.

çırpılmış scrambled.

çift porsiyon twice a single helping of food. Kebab houses, for example, often provide a choice in serving size.

çifte kavrulmuş shelled and twice-roasted pistachios.

çiğ raw.

çikolata chocolate.

çil partridge.

çilek strawberry.

çilek peltesi strawberry jelly.

çinakop fish similar to bluefish; see *lüfer*.

çips patates potato chips.

çipura a flat fish resembling pompano.

çiroz emaciated mackerel, caught after the spawning season, which are salted, sun-dried and eaten with dill.

çocuk yemekleri a child's menu.

çok şekerli very sweet.

çorba soup.

çorbacı soupmaker.

çorbalar the plural of soup. On menus, this word heads the soup section.

çökelek a soft cheese made from skim milk.

çömlek earthenware pot. The preparation of lamb and vegetables called *çömlek kebabı* is typically baked in the bottom portion of a red clay jug, after its neck and handle are broken off (see *Menu Guide*).

çörek a rich, flaky pastry made of lightly sweetened dough flavored with *mahleb*.

çörekotu black cumin seeds, also known as Russian caraway, which decorate the surface of many varieties of breads and rolls.

çulluk woodcock.

çupra porgy fish.

dağ çayı see *ada çayı*.

damla a drop.

FOODS & FLAVORS GUIDE

damla sakız see *sakız.*

dana calf; also called *buzağı.*

dana eti veal.

dara hindiba dandelion.

darı millet; also can mean corn kernals.

davar a term for small, food.animals such as sheep or goats.

defne yaprağı bay leaf.

değirmen unu whole wheat flour.

deniz marine or sea.

deniz mahsulleri seafood.

dere pisisi flounder.

dereotu dill.

dil tongue.

dil balığı sole.

dil peyniri string cheese.

doğranmış diced or chopped.

dolma stuffed or stuffed vegetable, etc. A typical stuffing is seasoned minced meat, rice, pine nuts and currants.

dolmalık biber see *yeşil biber.*

domates tomato.

domates salçası tomato sauce.

domates suyu tomato juice.

domuz pig. Pork will not be readily available because the Moslem religion forbids its consumption.

dondurma ice cream. The city of Kahramanmaraş, in southeastern Anatolia, is famous for its "elastic" ice cream. Powdered orchid root, or *sahleb*, an additive that thickens and flavors it, produces the taffy-like consistency. This special ice cream is sold by colorfully costumed vendors throughout Turkey who delight in showcasing the remarkable qualities of their product, sometimes with hilarious comedy routines.

döş breast or brisket; often implies mutton. Compare with *göğüs.*

dövme hulled whole wheat, which is used for soups and cereals. After cooking, it becomes plump and soft. This form of wheat is a main ingredient of *aşure*, a sweet pudding made of wheat, legumes, dried fruits and nuts (see *aşurelik buğday*, this *Guide* and the *Menu Guide*).

dövülmemiş biber peppercorn; also called *biber tanesi.*

dubar striped gray mullet.

duble double portion. This term refers to drinks, rather than to food.

durakı nectarine; also called *tüysüz şeftalı.*

dut mulberry.

düğü finely ground bulgar; also called *ince bulgur.*

dürüm a piece of bread used to pick up food; also the name of a hot sandwich and a dessert (see *Menu Guide*).

ekmek bread.

ekmek kadayıfı a special, round, bread-like dough available commercially, which is the basis for the syrup-soaked dessert of the same name (see *Menu Guide*).

ekmek sepeti basket of bread.

ekşi sour.

ekşi elma sour apple.

elma apple.

elma şarabı cider.

enginar artichoke.

erik plum.

erik pestili dark-colored sheet of dried plums, usually rolled up like a jelly roll.

erişte homemade noodles.

eski old or aged.

eski yağlı kaşar aged *kaşar* cheese with a firm, oily (meaning not dry) texture.

esmer bira dark beer; also called *siyah bira.*

esnaf lokantası a restaurant primarily serving dishes prepared ahead of time and kept warm. It tends to be located in busy market areas. Neighboring shopkeepers and craftspeople, who typically frequent these establishments, are able to get hearty, home-style cooking cheaply and fast.

et meat.

et suyu consommé.

etimek a type of cracker.

etler the plural of meat. On menus, this word heads the meat section.

ezme purée or paste.

fasulye bean.

fesleğen sweet basil; also called *reyhan* and *basılıkum.*

fıçı birası draft beer.

fındık hazelnut or filbert.

fırık roasted or sun-dried, unripe wheat.

fırın oven, oven-roasted or baked.

fırında baked.

fıstık nut.

FOODS & FLAVORS GUIDE

fileto fillet.

fincan cup.

fincan tabağı saucer.

francala a loaf of white bread.

Frenk elması loquat, a yellow plum-like fruit.

Frenk maydanozu chervil.

Frenk salatası chicory or endive; also called *radike* or *hindiba.*

Frenk sarımsağı chive; also called *yaban sarımsağı.*

Frenk üzümü red currant; also called *kuş üzümü.*

füme smoked; another term for this is *tütsülenmiş.*

galeta breadstick, rusk or bread crumbs.

garson waiter.

gazino an establishment combining dining and family entertainment in a setting where alcoholic beverages are available, in contrast to *aile gazinosu* where alcohol is not available.

gazoz soda pop.

gelincik tohumu poppy seed; also called *haşhaş tohumu.*

gerdan neck.

gevrek biscuit or cracker.

geyik deer.

geyik otu savory.

gıda nutrition.

gıda pazarı supermarket.

gofret waffle or wafer. Also the name of a confection made with chocolate and wafers.

göğüs breast meat; generally refers to chicken. Compare with *döş.*

gömmeç the method of baking bread in embers; also called *kümeç.*

gravyer type of Swiss-like cheese.

greyfrut see *altıntop.*

güğüm a lidded copper pot with a handle and small pouring spout. It traditionally was kept on the stove so a supply of warm water for washing hands would always be available.

gül rose; its petals are used to flavor syrup and sherbet.

gül suyu rose water.

gül yaprağı rose petal.

güllaç a thin, rice flour wafer used to make the dessert of the same name (see *Menu Guide*).

gümüş balığı smelt; also called *çamuka.*

güneşte sun-cooked.

güveç an earthenware casserole. A strip of dough is used to seal its lid during cooking. It is also the name of a vegetable mixture sometimes containing meat, poultry or shrimp.

habbe grain; the plural form of the word is *hububat.*

ham unprocessed, unripe or green.

ham şeker brown sugar.

hamsi an anchovy-like fish, used fresh in numerous dishes. This fish is extremely popular in the Black Sea region.

hamur dough. At its simplest, it is a mixture of just flour and water, such as the tiny dough balls in *yuvarlama* (see *Menu Guide*) or the thread-like strands of *tel kadayif* (see this *Guide*).

hamur açma sofrası the low, round table at which Anatolian women traditionally sit and roll dough called *yufka* into thin sheets with a long, thin rolling pin called an *oklava.*

hardal mustard.

hardal tohumu mustard seed.

harnup carob; also called *keçi boynuzu.*

harnupiye a drink made from carob.

haspir safflower; also called *aspur.*

haşhaş tohumu poppyseed; also called *gelincik tohumu.*

haşlama boiled; another word for boiled is *kaynama.*

haşlanmış yumurta hard-boiled egg; also called *lop yumurta, hazırlop yumurta* and *katı yumurta.*

havuç carrot.

havyar caviar.

haya testicle. Also called *husye* and *yumurta.*

hazır yemek ready-to-go food.

hazırlop hard-boiled.

hazırlop yumurta hard-boiled egg; also called *haşlanmış yumurta.*

hedik boiled wheat.

helva (halvah) a dessert made with semolina, sesame paste or flour, mixed with sugar and nuts.

hesap the bill or check.

hespir safflower; also called *aspur.*

hıyar cucumber; also called *salatalık.*

hindi turkey.

FOODS & FLAVORS GUIDE

hindiba chickory or endive; also called Frenk *salatası.*

Hindistan cevizi coconut.

Hint safranı turmeric; also called *zerdeçal.*

hodan borage.

hoşaf a cold compote of small dried fruits such as grapes and apricots, stewed in sugar and water or in *pekmez,* the molasses made from grape juice. Less commonly, fresh fruit is used. A similar fruit mixture, called *komposto,* typically is made with fresh fruit rather than dried, and larger fruits such as peaches or pears are used.

hububat grains; see *habbe.*

hurma date.

hurma yağı palm oil.

husye testicle; also called *haya.*

hünnap Chinese date or common jujube.

ıhlamur linden blossom; also a tea made from linden blossoms, which is sweetened with sugar and often flavored with cinnamon. It is considered a cold remedy.

ılık lukewarm.

ısga small onion.

ıspanak spinach.

ıspanak kökü spinach root.

ıstakoz lobster.

ışkın wild rhubarb.

ızgara grill or grilled.

ibrik ewer.

iç a generic word for giblets or offal, interior or inside, or a stuffing. Other words for giblets are *sakatat* and *takım.*

iç bakla shelled bean.

iç bezelye shelled pea.

içecek drink or beverage.

içecekler the plural of beverage. On menus, this word heads the beverage section.

içilir drinkable.

içilmez undrinkable.

içki drink, but connotes alcoholic drink.

içkili alcoholic beverages are available.

içkisiz no alcoholic beverages are available.

içli stuffed.

içme suyu drinking water.

iftar the meal at sundown during Ramadan.

ince fine, meaning small particles.

ince bulgur finely ground bulgur. Also called *simit and düğü bulgur.*

incik shank.

incir fig.

inek cow.

irmik semolina; it is a typical ingredient of halvah, or *helva.*

islim steamed.

ispendik small bass.

ispirto rubbing alcohol; compare with *alkollü içki.*

istavrit horse mackerel.

istridye oyster.

işkembe tripe.

işkembeci a restaurant specializing in *iskembe çorbası,* or mutton tripe soup, whose consumption is believed to ward off hangovers. It is often open all night!

işkine rock bass.

iyi pişmiş well-done. Another word for this is *pişkin.*

izmarit sea bream.

jambon ham. (Moslem law forbids eating any form of pork. Nevertheless, ham is available in some İstanbul delicatessens.)

jelatin gelatin; it is available as a powder or in sheets.

jöle jelly or Jello; another word for jelly is *pelte.*

kabak pumpkin or squash. The elongated, dark-green zucchini and light-green varieties of squash are most common. In addition to fresh squash sold in the markets, there are dried, hollowed-out ones, strung together on ropes, to make various stuffed dishes during winter. Another name for pumpkin is *bal kabağı;* for zucchini squash, *sakız kabağı.*

kabak çekirdeği pumpkin seed; see *çekirdek.*

kabuk rind, skin or shell.

kabuklu deniz hayvanları shellfish; also called *kabuklu deniz ürünü.*

kabuklu deniz ürünü see *kabuklu deniz hayvanları.*

kaburga rib.

kadayıf strands of griddle-fried dough; see *tel kadayıf.*

FOODS & FLAVORS GUIDE

kahvaltı breakfast.

kahve coffee. Finely pulverized beans are used to make Turkish coffee. It is brewed in a wide-mouthed, long-handled metal pot called a *cezve*.

kahve değirmeni coffee grinder.

kahve fincanı coffee cup.

kahve kaşığı coffee spoon.

kahveci coffee seller or coffee shop owner.

kahvehane coffee shop or café.

kak dried fruit.

kakaç dried and salted food; also called *tuzlanmış*.

kakao cocoa.

kakule cardamom.

kalamar squid; also called *mürekkep balığı* and *supya*.

kalinos perch.

kalkan turbot.

kanyak cognac or brandy.

kapari caper; also called *kebere*.

kaplıca small-grained wheat.

kara black. Another word for black is *siyah*.

kara biber black pepper.

kara ceviz black walnut.

kara ekmek black bread.

kara lâhana black cabbage.

karaciğer liver; also called *ciğer*.

karagöz black sea bream.

karamela caramel.

karanfil clove.

karavides freshwater crayfish; also spelled *kerevides*.

karaviye caraway.

karbonat baking powder.

karışık various, assorted, mixed; also called *çeşitli*.

karides shrimp.

karnıbahar cauliflower.

karpuz watermelon.

kasap butcher or butcher's shop.

kaşar peyniri a mild, yellow cheese made from sheep's milk.

kaşık spoon.

katı yumurta hard-boiled egg; also called *haşlanmış yumurta*.

katmerli hamur homemade dough for flaky pastries.

kavanoz jar or pot.

kavun melon.

kavurma fried or roasted; it also means fried or roasted meat. It is the name for a preparation of mutton, which traditionally was cooked, salted and preserved for winter use (see *Menu Guide*).

kaya balığı gurnard fish; also called *kırlangıç*.

kayısı apricot.

kayısı pestili sheet of dried apricots, usually rolled up like a jelly roll.

kayısı yumurta a boiled egg with firm egg white and a somewhat soft, but not runny, egg yolk.

kaymak thick cream traditionally made from buffalo milk. It is reduced by boiling until firm enough to slice, and is used as a dessert filling or accompaniment.

kaymak dondurması unflavored ice cream; also called *sade dondurma*.

kaz goose.

kazan a large soup kettle.

kâğıt grease-proof parchment paper used in cooking; also called *yağlı kâğıt*.

kâse bowl.

kebap pieces of meat cooked in many ways, especially roasted. All sorts of vegetables and fruits can be included in a dish and numerous regional variations exist. Meat cooked on a skewer (*şiş*) is called *şiş kebabı*. Many different types of food are considered *kebap*. Even roasted chestnuts and corn on the cob are included in this category. Usage of the term *kebap*, which originally meant meat turned over fire in the open air, has undergone considerable evolution.

kebap şişi skewer for kebabs; also just called *şiş*.

kebapçı a restaurant serving kebabs.

kebaplar the plural of kebab. On menus, this word heads the kebab section.

kebere caper; also called *kapari*.

keçi goat.

keçi boynuzu carob; also called *harnup*.

kefal gray mullet.

kek dry, bread-like cake.

kekik thyme.

keklik partridge.

kelek unripe melon.

kemer patlıcanı the common, long and slender variety of eggplant in Turkey.

kepek ekmek whole wheat bread.

kerevides freshwater crayfish; also spelled *karavides*.

kereviz celery or celery root.

kereviz tohumu celery seed.

kesik cheese curd.

kesilmiş curdled.

kesme makarna a type of flat noodle.

kesme şeker sugar cube.

kestane chestnut.

kestane kebap roasted chestnut.

kestane şekeri candied chestnut.

ketçap ketchup.

kete a cake made of rice flour.

kılıç balığı swordfish.

kıraathane a coffee house, where games such as backgammon frequently are played.

kırlangıç gurnard; also called *kaya balığı* and *taş balığı.*

kırmızı red.

kırmızı biber red pepper, paprika or cayenne pepper.

kırmızı mercimek red lentil.

kırmızı turp radish.

kış baharatı winter savory.

kıyma minced meat.

kızarmış ekmek toast.

kızartma browned in oil.

kızılcık a tart, scarlet berry known as the cornelian cherry.

kimyon cumin.

kinin quinine.

kiraz sweet cherry.

kiremit tile. Several dishes are baked on a clay tile or in a shallow clay dish to enhance the flavor.

kişniş coriander seed; also called *cere otu.*

koç ram.

koç başı ram's head.

koç yumurtası ram's testicle.

kofana fish similar to bluefish; see *lüfer.*

kol arm or shoulder.

kola cola.

kolyos Spanish mackerel.

komposto a cold compote made with large fresh fruit such as peaches or pears, which are stewed in sugar and water or *pekmez.* Less commonly, dried fruit is used. A similar concoction, the *hoşaf*, is made with smaller fruits, which typically are dried rather than fresh.

konserve bottled or canned food.

kontrfile beef steak.

konyak brandy or cognac.

koruk unripe grape.

koruk ekşisi vinegar made from unripe grapes, which is used sparingly to add a sour taste to certain foods such as salads.

koruk lüferi fish similar to blue fish; see *lüfer*.

koyun mutton.

koyun eti mutton meat.

köfte a round- or oblong-shaped patty of seasoned minced meat, typically lamb, cooked in various ways—fried, baked, grilled etc. Many regional variations exist; some include bulgur or rice and others are meatless. For certain preparations, a small handful of the mixture is pressed around a special broad, flat skewer into a sausage shape and then grilled.

köfteci seller of *köfte* or a restaurant specializing in *köfte*; also the name for street peddlers.

köfter candy made from boiled grape juice.

kök root.

köklü lahana kohlrabi.

kömür charcoal.

köpek balığı shark or dogfish.

közleme grilled on embers.

krem cream; also spelled *krema*; also called *süt başı*.

krem şantiye a thick cream resembling pastry cream.

krem şokola chocolate pudding.

krema see *krem*.

krikrak bread stick; it is thicker than the variety called *batonsale*.

kurabiye cookie.

kuru dry or dried.

kuru ekmek dry (stale) bread.

kuru erik prune.

kuru fasulye white bean.

kuru meyve dried fruit.

kuru üzüm raisin.

kuru yemiş dried fruit or nuts.

kurukahveci a store selling roasted and ground coffee beans, dried fruits and nuts.

kurut powdered milk; also called *süt tozu.*

kuskus couscous.

kuş üzümü red currant; also called Frenk *üzümü.*

kuşbaşı et cubes of meat for stewing.

kuşhane a wide, lidded cooking pan, which is somewhat deeper than the one called *sahan.*

kuşkonmaz asparagus.

kuver cover charge, which is equal to the cost of bread and water.

kuyruk yağı sheep's tail fat traditionally used in certain recipes.

kuzu lamb.

kuzu budu leg of lamb.

kuzu kulağı sorrel.

küçük small.

küçük ekmek bread roll.

küçük Hindistan cevizi nutmeg.

küflü çokelek a soft blue cheese; a speciality of İskenderun, a city in the Mediterranean region of Turkey.

kümeç method of baking bread in embers; also called *gömmeç.*

kümes hayvanları poultry.

kürek shoulder blade.

lâhana cabbage.

lâhana turşusu pickled cabbage.

lâkerda salted bonito.

lâkoz grouper.

lâpa soft, mushy porridge or stew, made of rice.

lâtilokum confection called Turkish delight; also called *lokum.*

lâvaş unleavened peasant bread made by rolling dough called *yufka* into thin sheets and browning them on a griddle. It is stored dried and softened with a light sprinkling of water before eating. Also called *yufka ekmeği.*

leblebi a snack of chickpeas, partially cooked and dried (the white variety) or roasted (the yellow variety).

leblebici seller of roasted chickpeas.

levrek sea bass.

likör liqueur.

limon lemon.

limonata lemonade.

lokanta restaurant; also called *restoran.*

lokantacı restaurateur.

lokum Turkish delight; a type of candy made with cornstarch, syrup, flavoring and various other ingredients such as nuts and dried fruits. Also called *lâtilokum*.

lop et boneless meat.

lop yumurta hard-boiled egg; also called *haşlanmış yumurta*.

lor peyniri soft, creamy goat cheese.

lüfer a fish indigenous to the Bosphorus, which is similar to the bluefish. It is highly prized by an *İstanbullu* (native of İstanbul). Different names are given to this fish, depending on its relative size, or age. *Çinakop* is a small, young fish. *Koruk lüferi* and *sarı kanat* refer to medium-size fish. *Kofana* is a large specimen.

mablak spatula or wooden spoon.

maden sodası carbonated mineral water.

maden suyu uncarbonated mineral water.

mahallebi see *muhallebi*.

mahleb the aromatic seeds of the black cherry, which are ground and added to rolls and sweet breads such as *çörek*. These small, beige seeds are available whole or ground.

mahun cevizi cashew.

makarna macaroni.

manav fruit seller or fruit store.

manda water buffalo.

mandalina tangerine.

mandıra dairy; less commonly called *süthane*.

mangal charcoal brazier.

mantar mushroom.

margarin margarine.

marmelat marmalade.

marul romaine lettuce.

mastika see *sakız*; also a type of resin-flavored wine.

maydanoz parsley.

mayhoş tart or sourish.

mayhoş elma a somewhat-sour apple.

mayonez mayonnaise.

melâs molasses.

menba suyu spring water.

FOODS & FLAVORS GUIDE

menekşe violet; its petals are used for flavoring syrup and sherbet.

mercan balığı red sea bream.

mercanköşk sweet majoram; also called *amarak.*

mercimek lentil; also called *yasmık.*

merdane rolling pin; also see *oklava.*

merlanos whiting; also called *mezit,* or *mezgit,* and *tavuk balığı.*

mersin balığı sturgeon.

meryemiye sage; also called *ada çayı.*

meşrubat soft drinks. On menus, the word *meşrubatlar* heads the soft drink section.

mevsim foods in season.

meyan balı licorice extract.

meyan kökü licorice root; also called *tatlı boyan.*

meyan şerbeti a drink made from licorice root.

meyhane bar or pub.

meyve fruit; also called *yemiş.*

meyve suyu fruit juice.

meyve şekerlemesi candied fruit.

meze appetizer; also called *çerez* and *ordövr.* Several appetizers traditionally accompany *rakı,* the national liquor of Turkey distilled from grapes. Expect big trays bearing a large assortment of choices.

mezeler the plural of *meze.* On menus, the word *mezeler* heads the appetizer section.

mezit (mezgit) whiting; also called *merlanos.*

mısır corn.

mısır unu cornmeal.

mısır yağı corn oil.

midye mussel.

misket limonu lime.

morina white sturgeon.

muhallebi milk pudding; also spelled *mahallebi.*

muhallebici a pudding shop. Pastries and some meat dishes are usually also available in pudding shops.

mutfak kitchen or cuisine.

mutfak takımı a set of kitchen utensils.

muz banana.

mücver fritter; often made of zucchini.

mürekkep balığı squid; also called *kalamar.*

nane mint or peppermint.

nar pomegranate.

nar çekirdeği pomegranate seed.

nar ekşisi sour pomegranate juice or syrup.

nar suyu pomegranate juice.

nar şurubu pomegranate syrup.

narenciye citrus fruit. Also called *turunç*, although this word generally refers to the bitter, Seville orange.

nohut unripe chickpeas, in the pod and still on the stem. They are sold on the streets as snacks.

nokul a roll.

ocak cooking stove.

oklava a long, narrow rolling pin used for rolling out thin sheets of pastry dough called *yufka*.

olgun ripe; also called *olmuş*.

olmamış unripe.

omlet omelette.

ordövr see *meze*.

orkinos tuna fish.

orta medium.

orta pişmiş medium-cooked.

orta şekerli medium-sweet.

ortaya literally means "[put it] in the middle." It implies a dish for all to eat, and generally refers to salads and appetizers.

otlu peynir an herbed cheese made with sheep's milk.

öğle yemeği lunch.

ölçü kabı measuring cup.

ölçü kaşığı measuring spoon.

ördek duck; also called *badi*.

paça trotter; also called *bakanak*.

palamut bonito.

pancar beet.

pandispanya sponge cake.

Foods & Flavors Guide

pane breaded and fried.

papağan balığı parrot fish.

papatya chamomile; also called *sarı papatya.*

Paskalya çöreği braided Easter bread.

pasta a pastry, tart or sweet, moist cake.

pastahane pastry shop.

pastırma dried, salted meat cured with a paste called *çemen*, which consists primarily of red pepper, fenugreek seeds and garlic.

patates potato.

patates kızartması French fries.

patlamış mısır popcorn.

patlıcan eggplant. In addition to the mounds of fresh eggplant available in the markets, there are hollowed-out and dried ones, strung together on long ropes, to make various stuffed eggplant dishes during winter.

pavurya large crab.

pazı chard; also called *yabani ıspanak.*

pazar market; it especially refers to a farmer's market held on the street on a specific day of the week and dismantled afterwards. Food is not necessarily the only type of item sold. Compare with *çarşı.*

peçete napkin.

pekmez a molasses-like syrup made by boiling grape juice until it is reduced. A thicker variety is called *bulama*. Both are used as sugar substitutes.

peksimet melba toast, or dry pastry.

pelte see *jöle.*

pembe şarap rosé wine; also called *roze.*

pestil a sheet of dried fruit pulp.

peynir cheese.

peynir şekeri a soft white candy flavored with bergamot.

peynir tatlısı cheesecake, unlike what we think of as cheesecake. There are several varieties, including syrup-soaked sponge cakes containing cheese and confections similar to *lokma,* which are eaten warm (see *Menu Guide*).

pırasa leek.

pide leavened flat bread; comes in many shapes, lengths and surface textures.

piknik picnic.

pilâki a dish stewed in olive oil and onions and served cold. This is a popular way to prepare dried beans.

pilâv (pilaf) a dish of rice or bulgur, often containing pine nuts, raisins or dried currants, and various other ingredients. Typically, the rice is gently fried before it is boiled.

pilâvlar the plural of cooked rice. On menus, this word heads the section containing pilafs.

piliç a young, tender chicken.

pirinç uncooked rice.

pirzola chop or cutlet. It is a thinner cut than ours.

pisi balığı brill.

pişkin well done; also called *iyi pişmiş.*

pişmaniye a white spun-sugar confection. Mounds of it are in cases in the outdoor markets.

ponçik a sweet bun filled with jam and sprinkled with powdered sugar.

porsiyon portion.

portakal orange.

portakal suyu orange juice.

porto port wine.

pul biber flakes of dried red pepper.

püre purée; it usually means mashed potatoes.

radike chickory or endive; also called Frenk *salatası.*

rafadan yumurta soft-boiled egg.

rakı the national liquor of Turkey; an anise-flavored, colorless distillation from grapes. When diluted with ice or water it turns milky white. It is called lion's milk because of its potency, but aficionados say that by drinking some *şalgam*, a beet, carrot and lemon juice concoction, on the side, this potency is reduced.

razakı a type of large white grape usually made into raisins.

raziyane fennel; also spelled *rezene.*

reçel jam.

reçete recipe.

restoran see *lokanta.*

reyhan sweet basil; also called *fesleğen.*

rezene fennel; also spelled *raziyane.*

rina stingray; also called *vatoz.*

ringa herring.

roka arugula.

rosto roast meat.

roze rosé wine; also called *pembe şarap.*

saç convex iron griddle resembling an inverted wok, which is used primarily for cooking over wood-fueled fires.

saç peyniri a white cheese formed into pencil-thick ropes. Note that *saç* also means hair.

sade simple, plain or unsweetened.

sade dondurma unflavored ice cream; also called *kaymak dondurması.*

safran saffron.

sahan a shallow cooking pan.

sahanda fried.

sahanda yumurta fried egg.

sahleb the powdered root of an orchid, which is used to thicken and flavor certain foods. Ice cream containing it has a remarkable elastic consistency (see *dondurma*, this *Guide*). *Sahleb* is also the name of a sweet milk drink made with this root powder. The concoction is boiled until thick, and drunk hot, with a little cinnamon sprinkled on top. Also spelled *salep.*

sahur a pre-dawn meal during the fast of Ramadan.

sakatat giblets; also called *iç.*

sakız the pale-yellow resin from an evergreen acacia tree native to the Mediterrean. It is sold in small chunks, which are pulverized and added as flavoring to sweet breads, milk puddings and ice cream. It can be chewed as gum. Other names for this resin are *damla* (drop) *sakız* and *mastika*. A different type of *sakız* called *yayla* (high-plateau) *sakız* is obtainable at high altitude plateaus in eastern Turkey. This version is very hard and is used primarily as gum, becoming softer with chewing. Pieces are stored under water to keep fresh.

sakız kabağı zucchini; also called *kabak.*

salam salami.

salamura pickled in brine or marinated.

salata salad.

salatalar the plural of salad. On menus, this word heads the salad section.

salatalık cucumber; also called *hıyar.*

salça sauce; it usually means tomato sauce.

salep see *sahleb.*

salmalık midye a mussel for stewing.

sandöviç sandwich.

sardalya sardine.

sarı yellow.

sarı balık yellow fish.

sarı göz a type of sea bream.

sarı hani jewfish.

sarı kanat fish similar to bluefish; see *lüfer.*

sarı kiraz yellow cherry.

sarı papatya camomile; also called *papatya.*

sarımsak garlic.

sarımsak dişi garlic clove.

sarışın bira light-colored beer.

sarma wrapped or wrapped vegetables; also called *sebze sarma.*

sarpa a type of sea bream.

sazan carp.

sebze vegetable; less commonly called *zerzevat.*

sebze sarma see *sarma.*

sebzeci vegetable seller; also called *zerzevatçı.*

sebzeler the plural of vegetable. On menus, this word heads the vegetable section.

sek dry (alcoholic beverages); e.g., a "dry" wine or a drink without water or ice.

semizotu purslane, a salad plant with fleshy leaves.

serin cool.

servis ücreti service charge.

sıcak hot.

sığır cattle.

sığır eti beef.

sıkılmış squeezed or pressed juice.

simit a ring-shaped roll coated with sesame seeds. It is one of the most popular street snacks in Turkey. It is also a name for finely ground bulgur.

sinarit a variety of sea bream.

sini a large, round metal dish used as a communal food bowl in some rural areas. It is set on a low table or on top of rugs on the floor. Eaters sit around the bowl and take individual bites of food from it with a traditional wooden spoon.

sirke vinegar.

sivri biber a long, pointed green pepper. It can range in pungency from hot to mild.

siyah black; another word for black is *kara.*

siyah bira dark beer; also called *esmer bira.*

siyah turp a radish with a dark exterior and white flesh.

siyah zeytin black olive.

smetana sour cream.

soğan onion.

soğuk cold.

sokum a rump cut of meat.

som balığı salmon.

somun loaf (of bread).

sos dressing, sauce or gravy.

sosis sausage or hot dog.

sosisli sandöviç hot dog in a bun.

soya soybean.

söğüş boiled meat served cold.

su water.

su kabağı gourd.

su teresi watercress; also called *tere.*

sucuk a spicy sausage. Also the name for a confection made of walnuts strung together and then dunked several times in *pekmez*, the molasses-like mixture made by boiling grape juice, until the nut core is encased in a thick coating. This confection is also called *bandırma.*

sultani seedless grape; also called *çekirdeksiz üzüm.*

sulu watery or juicy.

sulu yemek stew; home-cooking.

sulu yemekler the plural of stew. On menus, this word heads the section containing stews.

sumak dried, ground berries from an edible variety of sumac shrub. This spice has a tart, lemony flavor and is commonly sprinkled on top of many foods, especially kebabs. Historically, it was used for its tartness before the arrival of lemons from Europe. Many restaurants will have it as a tabletop condiment.

supya squid; also called *kalamar.*

susam sesame seed.

susam yağı sesame seed oil.

suyu juice.

sülün pheasant.

sürahi pitcher or carafe.

süt milk.

süt başı see *krem.*

süt işi milk pudding.

süt kuzusu suckling lamb.

süt tozu powdered milk; also called *kurut.*

süthane dairy; also called *mandıra.*

sütlü kahve coffee with cream.

sütlü kakao milk chocolate.

süzme a thick yogurt made by straining the whey through cloth; also called *torba yoğurdu.*

şakıt moray eel or lamprey.

şalgam beet or turnip. Also the name of a drink (see *Menu Guide*).

şamama musk melon.

Şamfıstığı (nut of Damascus) pistachio; also called *Antep fıstığı*, or nut of Antep. The city of Antep, now Gaziantep, is the pistachio capital of Turkey.

şampanya champagne.

şarap wine.

şarapçı wine seller.

şarküteri delicatessen or charcuterie.

şef chief or head (not chef). Diners trying to get the attention of a waiter often shout "şef!"

şeftali peach.

şehriye vermicelli.

şeker sugar.

şeker pancarı sugarbeet.

şekerci confectioner, candy seller, or candymaker. Also called *şekerlemeci*.

şekerleme candy.

şekerlemeci see *şekerci*.

şekerli sugared or very sweet.

şekersiz unsweetened.

şerbet a cold, sweet drink, which is usually fruit-based; also means sherbet.

şerbetçi sherbet seller.

şıra a drink made from grape juice.

şırlağan sesame seed oil; also called *susam yağı*.

şile sweet majoram; also called *amarak*.

şiş skewer for kebabs; also called *kebap şişi*.

şişe bottle.

şişe suyu bottled water.

şişek a lamb yearling.

şurup syrup.

tabak plate.

tahıl cereal.

tahin a paste made from ground sesame seeds.

takım giblets; also called *iç*.

taksim çatalı serving fork.

taksim kaşığı serving spoon.

tandır a clay-lined oven or pit for cooking.

Foods & Flavors Guide

tarak scallop.

tarama dried, salted roe of the grey mullet, or an appetizer made from it.

taranga bream.

tarator a ground nut sauce containing garlic and vinegar or lemon juice. It accompanies several foods, especially fried mussels.

tarçın cinnamon.

tarhana a soup base made from a preparation of flour, yeast, tomatoes and red peppers, which is fermented, dried, pulverized and stored at room temperature. It is reconstitued in water or broth to make a soup called *tarhana çorbası* (see *Menu Guide*).

tarhun tarragon.

tas bowl or cup.

taş bademi wild almond.

taş balığı gurnard; also called *kırlangıç*.

taş kadayıf crumpet-like pancake; see *yassı kadayıf.*

taşım bring to a boil.

tat taste or flavor.

tatlı candy or confection.

tatlı acı bittersweet.

tatlı boyan licorice root; also called *meyan kökü.*

tatlı kırmızı biber sweet red pepper.

tatlı su drinking water.

tatlıca slightly sweet.

tatlılar the plural of sweetmeat or dessert. On menus, this word is found at the head of the desserts and confections section.

tava frying pan; also means food that has been breaded and deep-fried.

tavşan rabbit.

tavuk stewing hen.

tavuk balığı whiting; also called *merlanos.*

tavuk sakatatı chicken giblets.

taze fresh.

taze badem fresh almond. Street vendors sell delicious fresh almonds, which are kept cold on top of ice. The skin is gently rubbed off before eating the nutmeat.

taze fasulye green bean.

taze incir fresh fig.

taze soğan scallion.

tekir red mullet; see *barbunya.*

tel kadayıf delicate strands of griddle-fried dough made of flour and water, which are gathered from the griddle in large handfuls when done. These commercially available strands, resembling bundles of shredded wheat, are the basis for several desserts, including one of the same name (see *Menu Guide*). Also simply called *kadayıf.*

teleme a type of unsalted cheese.

tencere saucepan.

tencerede pişmiş cooked in a *tencere.*

tepsi a tray or baking tin, especially for making sweets like *baklava.* These trays are also used to make tray kebabs, or *tepsi kebabı* (see *Menu Guide*).

terbiye lemon and egg yolk sauce used for both flavoring and thickening.

tere watercress; also called *su teresi.*

tereyağı butter.

testi pitcher or jug.

testi peyniri a cheese, often mixed with herbs, which is aged for a year in a ceramic jug.

tirsi shad.

tohum seed; also called *çekirdek.*

ton balığı tunafish.

tonik tonic.

topatan kavunu an oval, yellow melon.

torba yoğurdu thick yogurt; see *süzme.*

torik bonito.

torta a fruit pie or tort; also spelled *turta.*

tortalar the plural of fruit tart. On menus, this word heads the fruit tart and pie section.

tost grilled cheese sandwich, a popular street snack made in special toasting machines that form ridges on the surface on the bread. Note that it does not mean toast, which is *kızarmış ekmek.*

toz şeker powdered sugar.

trança halibut.

tranş roundsteak.

tulum peyniri a sharp and salty goat's or sheep's cheese aged in a goat hide *(tulum).*

turna needlefish or pike.

turp radish.

turşu pickle or pickled.

turta see *torta.*

turunç citrus fruit; also called *narenciye.*

tuz salt.

tuzlanmış dried and salted food; also called *kakaç.*

tuzlu with salt.

tuzlu bisküvi salty cracker.
tuzlu yoğurt salted yogurt.
tuzluk salt shaker.
tuzsuz saltless.
tükenmez a type of fruit syrup.
tütsülenmiş smoked; also called *füme.*
tüysüz şeftalı nectarine; also called *durakı.*

ufak small.
un flour.
usare squeezed juice, essence or concentrate.
uskumru mackerel.
uykuluk sweetbreads (pancreas).

ütme roasted fresh corn or wheat.
üzüm grape.
üzüm suyu grape juice.

vanilya vanilla.
vatoz stingray; also called *rina.*
vergi tax.
vermut vermouth.
viski whiskey.
vişne morello cherry, a type of sour cherry with a dark-red skin.
vonoz small (young) mackerel.
votka vodka.

yaban wild.
yaban domuzu wild boar.
yaban sarımsağı chive; also called Frenk *sarımsağı.*
yaban turpu horseradish.
yabani amarak oregano.
yabani havuç parsnip.
yabani ıspanak chard; also called *pazı.*
yabani kaz wild goose.

yabani ördek wild duck.

yağ oil, fat, butter or grease.

yağlı kâğıt grease-proof parchment for cooking; also called *kâğıt.*

yağlı peynir an oily (meaning not dry) cheese.

yahni ragout.

yalancı (liar) dolma meatless, rice-stuffed grape leaves, which outwardly look like meat-filled ones.

yaprak leaf; also see *asma yaprağı.*

yarık kuru bezelye split pea.

yarım half.

yarım porsiyon half a regular-size portion. Kebab houses, for example, often provide a choice in serving size.

yarma coarsely ground wheat. It is cracked wheat, not bulgur.

yasemin jasmine flower, which is used to flavor certain foods such as ice cream and sherbet.

yasmık lentil; also called *mercimek.*

yassı flat or smooth.

yassı kadayıf a flat, crumpet-like pancake available commercially, which is the basis for the dessert of the same name. Also called *taş* (stone) *kadayıf* and *Arap* (or *Arab*) *kadayıfı* (see *Menu Guide*).

yaşmaklı yumurta poached egg.

yavan plain, dry or tasteless.

yayık ayranı buttermilk.

yayla sakızı see *sakız.*

yaz summer.

yemek food.

yemek listesi menu.

yemiş fruit; also called *meyve.*

yengeç crab; also called *çağanoz.*

yenibahar allspice.

yenir edible.

yenmez inedible.

yerfıstığı peanut; also called *Amerikan fıstığı.*

yeşil green.

yeşil biber green bell pepper; also called *dolmalık biber* (a pepper for dolmas).

yeşil zeytin green olive.

yılan balığı eel.

yoğurt yogurt. This ancient food, a product of milk curdled by a specific culture of bacteria, is an ubiquitous ingredient of Turkish cuisine.

Foods & Flavors Guide

yufka any of various hand-rolled doughs used in making pastries such as *börek* and *gözleme* (see *Menu Guide*).

yufka ekmeği unleavened peasant bread; also called *lavaş*.

yulaf oat.

yumurta egg; also a word for testicle. See *haya*.

yumurta akı egg white.

yumurta sarısı egg yolk.

yumurtalar the plural of egg. On menus, this word heads the egg section.

yürek heart.

yüz elli gram 150 grams, or a normal-size meal. Note that certain dishes are purchased by weight.

yüz gram 100 grams, or a small-size meal. Note that certain dishes are purchased by weight.

zargana garfish.

zencefil ginger.

zerdali wild apricot.

zerdeçal turmeric; also called *hint safranı*.

zerzevat vegetable; also called *sebze*.

zerzevatçı vegetable seller; also called *sebzeci*.

zeytin olive; usually implies the black one, which is much more common than the green olive.

zeytinyağı olive oil.

zeytinyağlı a meatless dish cooked with olive oil and served cold.

zeytinyağlılar the plural of a meatless dish cooked in olive oil and served cold. On menus, this word heads the section containing such dishes.

ziyafet banquet.

Bibliography

Ahmad, Feroz. *The Making of Modern Turkey*. London: Routledge, 1993.

Algar, Ayla. *Classical Turkish Cooking: Traditional Turkish Food for the American Kitchen*. New York: HarperCollins Publishers, 1991.

Algar, Ayla. Food in the Life of the Tekke. In *The Dervish Lodge: Architecture, Art, and Sufism in Ottoman Turkey*, edited by Raymond Lifchez, pp. 296–303. Berkeley, CA: University of California Press, 1992.

Ash, John. *A Byzantine Journey*. New York: Random House, 1995.

Brosnahan, Tom. *Turkey: A Travel Survival Kit,* 4th edition. Victoria, Australia: Lonely Planet, 1993.

Chase, Holly. *Turkish Tapestry: A Traveller's Portrait of Turkey*. Groton Long Point, CT: Bosphorus Books, 1993.

Davidson, Alan. *Seafood: A Connoisseur's Guide and Cookbook*. New York: Simon and Schuster, 1989.

Devrim, Shirin. *A Turkish Tapestry: The Shakirs of İstanbul*. London: Quartet Books, 1994.

Eren, Neşet. *The Art of Turkish Cooking or, Delectable Delights of Topkapı.* Garden City, New York: Doubleday & Company, Inc., 1969.

Faroqhi, Suraiya. *Towns and Townsmen of Ottoman Anatolia: Trade, Crafts and Food Production in an Urban Setting, 1520-1650*. Cambridge, England: Cambridge University Press, 1984.

Freely, John. *The Companion Guide to Turkey*. Englewood Cliffs, New Jersey: Prentice-Hall, Inc., 1984.

Goldstein, Joyce. *Mediterranean the Beautiful Cookbook: Authentic Recipes from the Mediterranean Lands*. San Francisco, California: Collins Publishers, 1994.

Hattox, Ralph S. *Coffee and Coffeehouses: The Origins of a Social Beverage in Medieval Near East*. Seattle, Washington: The University of Washington Press, 1985.

Kut, A. Turgut. *Açıklamalı Yemek Kitapları Bibliyografyası (Eski Harfli Yazma ve Basma Eserler)*. Ankara, Turkey: Kültür ve Turizm Bakanlığı, 1985.

Lewis, Geoffrey. *Turkey,* 3rd edition. New York: Frederick A. Praeger, Publishers, 1965.

Lewis, Raphaela. *Everyday Life in Ottoman Turkey*. London: B.T. Batsford Ltd, 1971.

Makal, Mahmut. *A Village in Anatolia*. London: Vallentine, Mitchell & Co. Ltd, 1954.

Mansel, Philip. *Sultans in Splendor*. New York: The Vendome Press, 1988.

Nickles, Harry G. *Middle Eastern Cooking*. New York: Time-Life Books, 1969.

Orga, Irfan. *Portrait of a Turkish Family,* 2nd edition. London: Eland, 1988

Orga, Irfan. *Turkish Cooking*. New York: The Citadel Press, 1958.

Perry, Charles. Grain Foods of the Early Turks. In *Food in Motion: The Migration of Foodstuffs and Cookery Techniques,* edited by Alan Davidson, pp. 11–22. Proceedings Oxford Symposium. Leeds, England: Prospect Books Ltd, 1983.

Ramazanoğlu, Gülseren. *Turkish Cooking,* 2nd edition. İstanbul, Turkey: Ramazanoğlu Publications, 1992.

Riza, Ali. *The Land and People of Turkey*. New York: The Macmillan Company, 1958.

Schick, Irvin C. and Ertuğrul Ahmet Tonak, editors. *Turkey in Transition: New Perspectives*. Oxford: Oxford University Press, 1987.

Settle, Mary Lee. *Turkish Reflections: A Biography of a Place*. New York: Prentice Hall Press, 1991.

Stoneman, Richard. *A Travellers's History of Turkey*. Brooklyn, New York: Interlink Books, 1993.

Weiker, Walter F. *The Modernization of Turkey: From Ataturk to the Present Day*. New York: Holmes & Meier Publishers, Inc., 1981.

Wheatcroft, Andrew. *The Ottomans*. London: Viking, 1993.

Wolfert, Paula. *The Cooking of the Eastern Mediterranean*. New York: HarperCollins Publishers, 1994.

Yasgan, Mehmet, editor. *Specialities of Turkish Cuisine*. İstanbul, Turkey: Yazgan Turizm Tic. Ltd. Şti., 1988.

Yeğen, Ekrem Muhittin. *Alaturka-Alafranga Tatlı-Pasta Öğretimi ve Soğuk Yemekler-Mezeler-Salatalar,* 16th revised edition. (Turkish and Western Desserts-Cakes and Cold Dishes-Appetizers-Salads.) İstanbul: İnkılâp Kitabevi, 1992.

Yeğen, Ekrem Muhittin. *Alaturka-Alafranga Yemek Öğretimi ve Sofra Düzeni-Sofra Görgüsü,* 20th revised edition. (Turkish and Western Cookery and Table Setting-Etiquette.) İstanbul: İnkılâp Kitabevi, 1994.

Yurtsever, Tunçay. *The Famous Turkish Cookery*. İstanbul, Turkey: Minyatür Yayınları, n.d.

Zürcher, Erik J. Turkey: *A Modern History*. London: I.B. Tauris & Co. Ltd, 1994.

Index

ORDER FORM

Use this form to order additional copies of **Eat Smart in India** or to order any of the other fine guidebooks in the **EAT SMART** (How to Decipher the Menu, Know the Market Foods and Embark on a Tasting Adventure) series.

Please send me:

_____ copies of **Eat Smart in Turkey (2nd Edition)** - $13.95

_____ copies of **Eat Smart in India** - $13.95

_____ copies of **Eat Smart in Brazil** - $12.95

_____ copies of **Eat Smart in Indonesia** - $12.95

_____ copies of **Eat Smart in Mexico** - $12.95

_____ copies of **Eat Smart in Morocco** - $12.95

_____ copies of **Eat Smart in Poland** - $12.95

Add $2.50 postage for one book, $1.00 for each additional book. Wisconsin residents add 5% sales tax. For international orders, please inquire about postal charges.

Check enclosed for $ _____

Please charge my: VISA_____ MASTERCARD_____

Card # _____ Exp. _____

Signature: _____

Name: _____

Address: _____

City: _____ State: _____ Zip: _____

Telephone: _____

Email: _____

Mail this form to:

Ginkgo Press, Inc.
2018 Chamberlain Ave.
Madison, Wisconsin 53726
Tel: 888-280-7060
Fax: 608-233-0053
http://www.ginkgopress.com
info@ginkgopress.com

NOTES

design   Ekeby
cover design   Susan P. Chwae
color printing   Widen Enterprises
text printing and binding   Sheridan Books, Inc.

typefaces   Garamond Simoncini and Helvetica Black
paper   60# White